Click And Connect

A Real-World Guide to Clicker Training for You and Your Pup

Pete Grant

Table of Contents

Introduction

Click and Connect: A Real-World Guide to Clicker Training for You and Your Pup

Hey there, fellow dog enthusiasts! If you've ever wished there was a universal remote for your furry friend, you're in for a treat - because clicker training is as close as it gets. Welcome to a click-and-connect type of dog training that will turn your dog's learning experience into a tail-wagging adventure.

Before you start worrying that this will be a complicated, lengthy, and frustrating process for both of you, let's take a step back. Clicker training is all about simplicity, communication, and a bowl full of positive vibes. With this guide, you'll only need ten minutes a day to dedicate to training. No need for advanced degrees or expensive professional training camps - just ten minutes and a willingness to connect with your pup in a fun, effective, and all-around heartwarming way.

In this book, we're ditching the fancy jargon and theories. Instead, we're diving into the nitty-gritty of clicker training - what it is, why it works, and how you can use it in your everyday life with your dog. Whether you're dealing with a bouncing ball of fluff or a seasoned, wise old-timer, this guide is your passport to a world where communication between you and your pup becomes as clear as a bell (or click, in this case).

Think of clicker training as a magical bridge between human and canine languages. It's the high-five your dog gives you when they finally grasp a new trick and the fist bump you'll want to share in return. We're not just talking about commands here; we're talking about a language of connection, understanding, and mutual celebration.

So, grab your clicker - that little plastic noisemaker is about to become your new best friend - and let's embark on a journey where learning is a two-way street, and every click brings you and your pup closer together. Get ready for a remarkable training experience that is simple and rewarding. It will make the ten minutes you spend dedicated to your pup's learning the highlight of your day.

There are many reasons dog owners choose clicker training for their pup. Clicker training provides a clear and distinct signal to mark the exact moment your dog performs the desired behavior. This instant feedback helps them understand which action earned the reward. The clicker allows for precise timing, which is crucial in dog training. Timing is everything regarding reinforcing behaviors, and the clicker helps you pinpoint the exact moment your dog does something right.

Besides providing clear and concise communication to your pup, clicker training makes the whole experience positive and rewarding. This is done through short, consistent training sessions focusing on positive reinforcement. Depending on your pups preference, the rewards for responding correctly to commands include treats, praise, and play. The rewards make the training something you and your pup will look forward to time and time again.

When it comes to learning something new, there is nothing more frustrating than mixed or mismatched information. Clicker training provides a consistent and unique sound that will be associated with a reward. This eliminates the chance for confusion and backtracking in the learning process. And when a pup doesn't know the right answer, they'll trial and error until they hear the click. Your pup will literally learn to problem-solve. This will increase their confidence in you as their leader and in themselves making them more willing to try new things.

The sound of the click, once associated with a reward, will grab your pup's attention very quickly. When fully focused on the task, they learn commands much more quickly. Faster learning means more opportunities for reward, growth in trust, and development of a special bond between the dog and their trainer.

Lastly, clicker training is just plain fun! No complicated and time-consuming programs that bore and turn into a chore. This engaging and playful learning style for your pup will create special memories and experiences for years to come. Remember, while the clicker training program is a fantastic learning tool, it takes teaching and learning along with your canine companion!

Chapter 1:

Introduction to Clicker Training

Welcome to the world of clicker training, where the 'click' of a small device holds the key to unlocking a language of positive communication with your canine companion. In this chapter, we'll delve into the origins and evolution of clicker training, exploring how a simple click has become a powerful tool for building strong bonds between humans and their furry friends. Throughout the book, you'll come to realize that training is a dynamic and ongoing process that benefits both you and your dog. It's a key component of responsible dog ownership, contributing to a positive and mutually rewarding relationship.

Training your dog is important for various reasons, and it contributes to a harmonious and fulfilling relationship between the pup and the owner. First and foremost, properly trained pups are less likely to engage in risky behaviors or put themselves in dangerous situations. Basic commands such as "sit," "stay," and "come" can be crucial for keeping your dog safe in a variety of environments. Training your pup also helps them become more social and well-mannered around other people and other animals. A properly socialized dog is more likely to be comfortable and calm in various situations, reducing the risk of aggressive behavior. Also, training is a proactive approach to avoiding problem behaviors. You can reduce the likelihood of issues such as excessive barking, destructive chewing, or aggression. It provides mental stimulation to your pup as well as physical and can prevent boredom. A well-trained dog will be more welcome in public spaces, including parks, cafes, and pet-friendly events. This inclusivity allows owners to enjoy a wider range of activities with their dogs. All of a sudden, vet visits become easier and less stressful for your pup, too. They will build confidence in unknown environments because they trust that you have everything under control, and trust is built in your relationship. Overall, training your pup provides a higher quality of life that doesn't exist without the bond and trust that training provides. It allows you to enjoy each other to the fullest extent possible.

What is Clicker Training?

Clicker training is a positive reinforcement-based method used in dog training (and other animal training) that employs a small handheld device called a clicker. The clicker is a simple tool that makes a distinct clicking sound when pressed. The basic premise of clicker training is to use this sound as a precise and consistent marker to communicate to your dog when they have performed the desired behavior.

Before using the clicker for training, it is important to "charge the clicker" by clicking the device and then immediately following up with a treat for your pup. This creates a positive association with the clicker's noise and teaches your dog that a treat will soon follow. That way when they perform the desired behavior during training, the clicker can be used at the exact moment of success and rewarded promptly. The key here is consistency and precision.

Clicker training is versatile and can be used to teach a wide range of behaviors, from basic commands to more advanced tricks. It's known as a gentle and effective method that enhances communication between dogs and their owners while fostering a positive and enjoyable training experience. With consistency and patience, clicker training can contribute to a well-behaved and happy canine companion.

This method will allow you to witness the transformation of your dog's confidence as they master new skills through clicker training. Successive clicks and rewards boost their self-assurance and confidence, creating a happy canine partner who approaches new challenges with enthusiasm and a wagging tail. The reward system piques curiosity about what else they can do to receive a tasty morsel. They start looking for opportunities to hear that click, and when they do, they'll revert to the behavior that got it for them. This is how the commands and exercises are engrained initially. It just takes the initial curiosity to get them started, and then they're hooked. They'll be happy to please you, and they'll be happy to do what it takes to receive a bit of yummy liver, an organic homemade dog biscuit, or a bit of leftover chicken from the night before. The options are endless, and so are the benefits!

The History of Clicker Training

Between 1940 and 1950, a behaviorist named B.F. Skinner developed the foundation for understanding operant conditioning. Operant conditioning is a form of learning in which consequences strengthen or weaken behavior. Skinner's studies with pigeons and rats demonstrated the effectiveness of using positive reinforcement to shape behavior. Then, between 1960 and 1970, clicker training started its official roots with training dolphins. Trainers began using whistles as their reinforcement markers and this concept served as the basis of clicker training. In the 1990s, a behavioral biologist named Karen Pryor developed and popularized the dog training method known as clicker training, in which operant conditioning is leveraged through the sound of the device and the immediate reward when a desired behavior is performed.

Why Clicker Training Works

Clicker training works because it capitalizes on the principles of positive reinforcement, clear communication, and the psychology of learning in animals. It transforms the training process into a positive and enjoyable experience for the owner and their dog, resulting in effective and lasting behavior. This training method leverages precision and communication, instant feedback, positive reinforcement, conditional reinforcement (charging the clicker), versatility and mobility of training anywhere, promotes problem-solving and reduces stress and fear in your pup. The best part is that it creates and strengthens a strong bond between a dog and their owner due to the positive association of the training sessions.

The Clicker Connection

The clicker is a unique training tool for dogs because it is devoid of emotions and carries no fluctuations, tone, or mood that a human voice might. Its neutrality helps maintain consistency in communication. Because the clicker's sound is so non-specific, anyone in the family can help train your pup as long as they are consistent with the positive reward. This reduces the stress of the handler because they can deliver the same training experience to the pup and reap the same benefits. The training tool is small enough to fit in a pocket and can be utilized in various environments. This is great because it allows real-world situations to become part of the learning experience. With a properly conditioned clicker, you can grab your pup's attention quickly, making them more attentive to your cues. With the conditioning of the clicker, all of a sudden, this unassuming noise becomes an unmistakable signal that all is right with the world. Your pup is then praised or rewarded and happy as a clam.

The Basics of Positive Reinforcement

Dogs are simple creatures that value food, praise, and toys. That's why they have partnered with humans for companionship. We also love these things! When it comes to dishing out a reward for the behaviors we're looking for in our dogs, any of these benefits will work. The trick is getting the timing of the reward just right so that it is immediately associated with good behavior. This can be just a bit more difficult to do with a toy. Praise is a great way to reward your pup, but it takes time. For clicker training, treats work wonders because they can be given quickly and without the diversion of attention or focus of the exercise. Once the behavior is learned, praise should replace the treat so that treats are reserved for learning new things. This is harder than doing what they know is expected.

Positive reinforcement can be used at every possible opportunity. The more consistent the reward system, the better. The reward does not have to come directly after a command. It could potentially come when your pup exhibits a desired behavior all on its own. For instance, they come to you and sit. This can immediately be followed up with a click and reward. It will tell your pup that you love them coming to you and sitting versus running up to you and jumping.

A major "no-no" in positive reinforcement is using punishment or negative consequences during the training sessions. These can create a negative association with the experience and foster fear and mistrust. Negative associations during training can also confuse your pup, which will muddy the communication "waters." Best to keep the sessions short, intentional, and positive.

Chapter 2:

Getting Started

So, you've decided to start your journey with training your dog and want to know where to begin. The nice thing about clicker training is that you can introduce it at any point throughout a dog's lifespan. But there's no better time than now to begin the journey to come. First, you'll want to get your mind in the right space. Be ready to dedicate ten minutes a day to focused training with your pup, but don't forget to be an opportunist for good behavior rewards. I'll start by suggesting wearing clothes with pockets. One pocket for treats (a bit of kibble does just fine here) and another pocket for the clicker. It doesn't hurt to have more than one clicker stashed in the usual places that your pup frequents. That way, you always have training tools at your fingertips.

As you move throughout your training journey, embrace a learning mindset. Approach each training session with a positive attitude with a willingness to learn. Be willing to try new approaches and adjust your methods based on your dog's responses. Make sure that when you choose to start a training session, there won't be interruptions or distractions. After all, it is only ten minutes! As you go along and your dog becomes more skilled, you'll be able to train under all sorts of circumstances. But in the beginning, it's best to keep it short, focused, simple, and most of all, positive.

Necessary Equipment

- **The Clicker** - We recommend buying a few of these just in case one is lost, another family member wishes to partake in training as well, or to have stashed in all the usual spots for "Spot." Most pet shops will have clickers available, but if you can't find one locally, purchasing online is easy, too. Online pet shops or variety shops (such as Amazon) will also have clickers available. If you buy multiple clickers, buying the same brand and type might be best to avoid any slight variance in sound. You're ready to start once you have your clicker, this book, and your rewards!

- **Rewards** - All sorts of rewards work well as motivators for pups. However, when it comes to leveraging a focused training session, time is of the essence. We don't want them to get distracted or go dilly over full-body rubs and high-pitched praise. Treats work best in the beginning because they are quick and to the point. Later, when the behaviors are reward-worthy but practiced and conditioned, praise is the perfect way to say "thank you for remembering your manners." Funny enough, different pups have different preferences when it comes to treats. Also, some treats can be full of not-so-healthy ingredients and/or tremendously expensive. If you want to pop down to the organic, homemade puppy café' for some exorbitantly expensive treats, by all means! For the penny pincher, pieces of their regular dry kibble meals work just fine. Use whatever you know your pup loves, but keep it simple enough to stuff in your pocket.

Preparing for Training

For the first few sessions, seek out a space for training (your garage, backyard, spare room, or patio) that is void of distractions. Let the family, roommates, and anyone else know that these next ten minutes are for you and your pup - do not disturb. Set aside time consistently for ten minutes in the same spot to start the training. Have your clicker at hand and your treats readily accessible. Be ready to enjoy yourself and know that every day is a work in progress. Some days will be better than others, but you can always feel good about putting the time and energy into a relationship that will reward you tenfold.

In preparation for training, this next part is to read through the rest of this guide. Get to know the process you'll be embarking on and be comfortable with what's to come. Then, once you've read everything front-to-back, return to this second chapter to get started. The book will always be here for you to repeat a phase of the training, reference back when things get tough or confusing, or start from the beginning again when the next pup comes along. Because let's be honest, one pup is never enough!

Setting Training Goals

Give some thought about what you would like to accomplish with your dog. Would you like to simply know that you'll be able to stop them in their tracks if they're about to run out into the road? Or is this your first step to taking on agility competitions? Maybe you haven't thought about it just yet. That's okay. If you haven't, now is the time to set a few goals for yourself and your furry friend. What do you feel is a realistic goal given the time and dedication you plan to put into training your pup? While we only recommend training in ten-minute-per-day exercises, the extent of what you can eventually accomplish is endless.

In case you need some guidance around what types of goals are typical, easy starter goals, and realistic for a beginner dog trainer (that might be you), we've provided some examples:

- **Grooming** - Does your dog get nervous on the way to or at the groomer's? A goal for training might be that they stand still and allow the groomer to examine them, touch them, brush them, use clippers or scissors on their coat, and trim their nails.

- **Sitting or standing politely** - Does your dog get so excited to meet new people that they can't sit still? This is a great opportunity for training. Strangers should be able to say hello and even pet your dog without them jumping, running, and spinning around like a tornado.

- **React in a friendly and calm manner toward another dog** - This can be tricky. If a dog has had a bad experience in the past, there might be some ingrained aggressive or protective behavior to train away. However, applying clicker training here can change the quality of life for your pup drastically for the better.

- **Sit and stay** - There will be times when you need to be able to walk away from your dog and trust that they will stay put. If a ball rolls out into the road, imagine being able to tell them to sit and wait for you at the curb while you retrieve it. Training your dog to sit and stay could save their life one day.

- **Walk on a slack leash** - Their leash should stay slack when walking your dog. This means they respect you as the leader and focus on your initiatives. Dogs can develop bad habits of pulling on the leash or being distracted by the environment around them. This can be unsafe and unenjoyable for everyone.

- **Walk through busy public spaces** - While a pup should be able to walk on a slack leash, it should also be able to walk through a crowd without becoming overanxious or excitable. The goal is for them to remain calm and in control regardless of pedestrians.

- **Manage distractions** - Should there be a motorcycle that speeds by, a car backfiring, or loud children playing, a dog should be able to show interest without getting aggressive or barking excessively.

- **Come** - This is a basic command that can be trained early on with pups. The goal is that the dog comes quickly and consistently every time. This will assist in maintaining their focus as well as keeping themselves and others safe.

Safety Considerations

There are several safety considerations to consider when owning a dog many of which are related to training. First and foremost, we want to keep everyone from getting injured. Safety measures in place during training can protect your dog from physical harm during the session. Activities like agility training, jumping, or specific tricks can pose a risk if considerations are not considered, such as your pup's limitations and physical capabilities. Supervision is important during training especially if someone younger from the family will help out. It is possible for training equipment to be used incorrectly and result in an injury such as a strain, sprain, or something more severe.

Tips to Consider

- **Sticking to the Leash in Public** - Even a well-trained dog can have an off-day or an off-moment. When in public, it's safest to keep your dog on a leash to avoid a potential disaster from a moment of distraction.

- **Stay in Sight** - Even in areas considered safe for your dog to be off-leash, always keep them in sight. Remember that you are responsible for their safety and the safety of anyone they encounter.

- **Basic Training** - Not all pups are going to be agility stars, but they should be trained with the basic commands for safety purposes. Basic training for your pup is a community consideration and responsibility of every dog owner.

- **Food Safety** - Almost anything can become a treat and a motivation for dogs during training. However, it is important to be aware that some foods are very dangerous for dogs to eat. Potential toxins for pups can include avocados, onions, garlic, grapes, raisins, macadamia nuts, raw eggs, candy, and caffeine. (*10 Dog Safety Tips for 2021 | Sit Means Sit Dog Training Raleigh*, 2021)

- **Toys and Tears** - Look over all equipment, toys, and treats to be sure that everything is in proper condition before every training session. If a toy has a tear and any piece becomes a danger to the pup, it needs to be tossed out. Remember that a bad experience can have a very negative impact on future training sessions.

- **Run and Play** - Healthy dogs have lots of energy; just like humans, they can have difficulty focusing if they can't sit still. It's best to be proactive and get your dog out for some exercise! This will help stabilize their mood, energy levels, and focus in training.

- **Where's My Dog** - Consider getting a GPS tracker for your dog's collar. Dogs manage to get themselves lost all the time and not tracking them down can be devastating for a family or individual dog owner. A GPS can help you locate your dog more quickly and limit the time they are out alone.

- **Puppy-proofing** - This tip isn't strictly for puppies, but it all starts there, so we will, too. Puppies love to chew just about anything. That means that owners need to take a careful look around any space their pup (or full-grown dog that still loves to chew things) will inhabit and remove anything that could cause them harm if chewed. Examples include cords and cables, shoe laces, medications, Legos, hair elastics, trash bins, etc. I think you get the idea.

- **First Aid** - Compile a kit for your pup. There is no better protection than being proactive. Having a puppy's first aid kit on hand could save their life one day. Include a tissue cleaning solution, bandages, a thermometer, your dog's medical records, scissors, and styptic powder for an injured and bleeding nail.

- **Doggy Dental Care** - Examine your dog's teeth regularly and even give them a brush. Several items on the market can help keep your dog's teeth clean and free from gum disease and tooth decay, such as toothbrushes and paste or chewable treats that help scrape the grime away while they chew.

It is important to build trust with your animal throughout the training process. If a dog feels safe during a training session, they are more likely to engage willingly in the learning process and form positive associations with the sessions. When they trust their trainer, it leads to a feeling of emotional well-being and safety. This will reduce stress and anxiety in the pup and lead to a more pleasant process for everyone. Keeping the experience positive prevents fear or negative associations, which could lead to aggressiveness or injury.

Before starting your training program, consider your pup's overall health and age. Some training activities may be best to avoid so that injuries are not sustained. Tailoring the training program to your dog's needs is critical. Some exercises will be too strenuous for seniors, dogs with arthritis, or dogs recovering from other injuries. If you're ever unsure as to whether a training exercise is okay for your pup, consult your vet for advice.

If a training exercise seems to create a stressful environment for your pup or they begin to show aggressive behavior, then it may be best to avoid that particular training. They could be physically in pain or developing increased anxiety, and both of these situations could lead to injury in either the pup or the trainer. Again, consult a vet if you notice that a training session seems to be particularly aggravating to your dog.

Keeping your dog safe during training is fundamental to responsible and effective training. It prevents physical harm and nurtures a positive and trust-based relationship between you and your pup. Consistently safe training practices contribute to long-term health and a platform for lifelong learning.

Chapter 3:

Clicker Conditioning

It is a dog's nature to repeat an action that gets them the reward they sought. They're smarter than we give them credit for and will quickly learn the cause and effect of both a positive and negative nature. This is why clicker training must remain a positive experience at all costs. Once proper preparation and safety considerations have been taken; then it's time to get started in the first phase of training with a clicker called, Clicker Conditioning. We all know positive reinforcement is an effective training mechanism, but where does the clicker fit in? The clicker acts as a marker for good behavior. Hence, clicker training is also known as marker training. The clicker, or marker, is the conditioned reinforcement once it has been associated with a reward. Associating the clicker with a reward is critical to successful clicker training.

In a nutshell, clicker training is positive reinforcement training with the added benefit of precise communication. If you haven't already, give your clicker its first few clicks to become familiar with the sound it makes without your pup nearby. You'll notice that it makes a very quick and distinct sound that cannot be confused with any other day-to-day noises. And your pup delivers the noise the clicker makes consistent with every click. This means your pup delivers the same message whenever they hear the sound. It likely seems a very unassuming noise and doesn't possess any magical properties. However, once the clicker is conditioned, you may feel differently.

See, the problem with training with treats or other positive reinforcements without using some sort of marker for the desired behavior is that they may perform the desired action and then get immediately distracted by the excitement of the reward. Then, the message is confusing for them. Are you rewarding the moment that they sat when you said "sit"? Or are you rewarding the jump-up that they did when they saw you reach into your pocket for a treat? Rewarding your pup fast enough to deliver a clear message about what they are being rewarded for is almost impossible. Without a marker, your pup may not know the difference and continue to display both behaviors in hopes of being rewarded.

By following the clicker training methodology, you're choosing to communicate more effectively with your dog. They'll appreciate you for that and look forward to doing what you ask from them with the same efficiency. So, let's get started with the first step - charging the clicker.

Charging the Clicker

While you both enjoy the experience and bond, this part of this training methodology will make or break the success of what is to follow. If at any point you feel like the training is going a bit off course, you and your pup may benefit from another clicker charging session. This immediate and positive reinforcement conditioning will set the stage for an eager learning partner in your pup. If you've tried other training methods that didn't seem to get you the results you know your pup is capable of, the clicker conditioning will quickly set the stage for a canine partner that, all of a sudden, loves to learn. Communication between you and your dog will instantly elevate while you enjoy the experience and bond. To minimize distractions, begin the process in a quiet and familiar environment being built.

Steps to Charge the Clicker

1. **Choose a Quiet Environment** - To minimize distractions, begin the process in a quiet and familiar environment. This allows your dog to focus on the clicker sound and the association rewards.

2. **Gather the Treats** - Have a good supply of treats your dog finds particularly enticing. These treats will be used to reinforce the positive association with the clicker.

3. **Get Your Dog's Attention** - Ensure your dog is calm and ready to pay attention. Call your dog or wait until they naturally look at you.

4. Introduce the Clicker - Hold the clicker in one hand and have a treat ready in the other. Allow your dog to see and hear the clicker, but don't click it just yet.

5. Click and Reward - Click the clicker and immediately follow it with giving your pup a treat. The click and the treat should be almost simultaneous. This helps your dog associate the clicker sound with receiving a reward.

6. Repeat the Process - Repeat the click-and-reward process several times. Click, treat, click, treat. Keep the sessions short and positive. The goal is for your dog to make a clear connection between the clicker and getting a treat.

7. Observe Your Dog's Response - Watch for positive signs that your dog is making the association. This could include them looking at you expectantly or showing excitement when they hear the click.

8. Vary the Timing - Practice varying the timing between the click and the treat. Sometimes, click immediately; other times, wait a few seconds before delivering the treat. This helps your dog understand that the click predicts a reward.

9. Repetition and Consistency - Practice charging the clicker in multiple short sessions throughout the day. Consistency is key, so ensure that a reward follows each click. The more repetitions, the stronger the association becomes.

10. Generalization - Once your god readily responds to the clicker in a controlled environment, try using it in different locations or situations. This helps your dog generalize the association, understanding that the clicker means the same thing regardless of the context.

11. Gradual Progression - Gradually decrease the frequency of treating after the click as your dog becomes more familiar with the clicker. However, continue to reinforce with treats periodically to maintain the positive association.

By following these steps, you can effectively charge the clicker and lay the foundation for successful clicker training sessions with your dog.

Remember to keep the experience positive and enjoyable for your furry friend.

Timing and Consistency

Timing is key in clicker training because dogs learn through associative processes. Precise timing is critical because the closer the reward is to the behavior, the stronger the association your dog will make. Immediate feedback helps them connect their actions with the outcome. Dogs live in the present moment and operate on immediate feedback. So, the exact timing of rewards helps them understand which behavior is being reinforced. Timely rewards help your dog associate it with a specific command or behavior. This clarity aids in their understanding of what is expected during training. Rewarding a behavior immediately after it occurs increases the likelihood that the behavior will be repeated. This is especially important when teaching new commands or tricks. Precise timing also avoids confusion. Delayed rewards can result in your pup associating the reward with the wrong behavior, thus making it more challenging to understand what is expected. With timely rewards, trust is built, and in turn, confidence as well. They learn to rely on your cues and understand that their actions have a desired outcome, and when actioned, leads to a stronger bond between you and your dog.

Consistency can make or break the communication tool's effectiveness. Going through the process of conditioning, the clicker sets a foundation of clear expectations and trust between an owner and their dog. When the rewards stay consistent, your dog quickly learns what behaviors are desirable; then, their actions stay consistent as well. When the click is not always followed up with a treat, it sends mixed signals that can interrupt training progress. Your dog may find it difficult to discern whether what they did was positive or negative. When we're consistent with giving a reward directly after a click, it accelerates the learning process. Dogs thrive on routine and repetition. They love knowing what is going to happen next and being prepared for it. Predictability increases confidence in dogs, and consistent training provides a predictable structure that helps them feel at ease. Cues with timely responses strengthen the communication between you and your dog. They learn to trust your guidance when they can predict your reactions and the outcomes of their behaviors.

The Clicker as a Communication Tool

We've mentioned that clicker training is all about positive reinforcement and that the training sessions should be kept short, simple, and positive. For those who have tried other training methods in the past, it may seem negligent to dismiss consequential communication via constant positive reinforcement. Maybe this is counterintuitive because even pack leaders will correct members of the pack if they are out of line. So, what message do you send to your pup when they're misbehaving or not completing the task that is being asked of them? When it comes to clicker training, you would withhold the click. This may seem benign, but the goal of the communication method being introduced via this training method is that there is either a "right" or "wrong" answer/behavior to what is being asked. When there are only two communications to work with, it simplifies the learning process extensively.

With clicker training, the charging of the clicker creates a very easy and motivational path to follow. An easy path of trying to do what is asked and being rewarded the second it is performed drives dogs to keep trying, learn, try again, and, in the end, get it right. We'll ask for the same thing repeatedly and reward when the right thing is chosen again. Through this process, the wrong answers will be skipped entirely. They're a waste of time in getting to the goal of acknowledgment and a yummy treat.

It isn't entirely correct to say that there are no negative consequences to a dog's actions when training via the clicker method. It is important to keep the experience positive to maintain the pup's motivation to keep trying. However, there is a negative consequence for them should they not perform the asked behavior - they don't win the game. The positive reinforcement we can give in these situations is to go back to a command they know and will achieve easily so we can reward or break the command down into bite-sized pieces so your pup can try again with a smaller ask. Should all else fail, it is also okay to go back to charging the clicker to build that motivation and excitement up again.

Now that we understand how the foundation of the clicker training method works, we can move on to some of the basic training commands that every dog should know. Some of the commands may have already been learned via other training methods, but revisiting them via the clicker training method will only build confidence and a better training foundation between you and your pup. In the next chapter, we'll examine the commands that are the easiest to get started with and the most essential for responsible dog ownership.

Chapter 4:

Basic Obedience Commands

While going through the sets of basic obedience commands and their related steps in this chapter, remember that repetitive aspects will be involved, such as having the clicker and treats ready before beginning the process. It's true; we could assume that in reading this far in our clicker training guide, anyone would know that the clicker and the readily available treats are pertinent to the session's success. However, our goal with this guide is that at any point in time, a dog owner can pick up this training manual and flip to the exact set of steps they are looking to reference and have them 100% intact without having to jump to other sections, or even this chapter introduction, to be fully informed on the process. So, with that in mind, let's jump into the most common, beginner, but also most essential commands to start with in our clicker training methodology program. Just remember, limit the training sessions to 10 minutes, keep things simple, and enjoy rewarding your dog for all they are about to accomplish!

Sit

1. Have a clicker and some of your pup's favorite treats at the ready.

2. Go to a quiet and distraction-free environment.

3. Using their name, get your dog's attention.

4. Show your pup the clicker in your hand.

5. Wait for your pup to sit naturally. (If you have their attention and they're waiting for what's next, they will eventually sit on

their own accord.) The moment they sit, click the clicker and offer the treat.

6. Repeat step four to reinforce the desired behavior. If necessary, take a few steps to the right or left to encourage them to stand back up (they will likely want to follow where that tiny and delicious morsel has come from). As soon as they stand, stop moving and wait for them to sit again. Click and reward the sit immediately.

7. Continue to repeat step six, but now start adding the verbal cue "sit" as they sit. Again, immediately click the clicker and reward the behavior.

8. After completing steps five through seven various times, prompt a sit using the verbal cue "sit" without waiting for a natural sit. If necessary, you can use the treat to guide your dog into a sitting position and immediately click the clicker to reward your pup.

9. When your dog gets the hang of sitting on command, gradually increase the duration between when they sit and when you click the clicker and give them their treat. This will encourage them to stay in the sitting position longer.

10. Generalize the "sit" command by practicing in different locations. Repeat steps five through nine to remind them of your request. This will strengthen the association between the verbal command and the action they perform as they'll realize that it means the same thing regardless of their environment.

Down (or Lie Down)

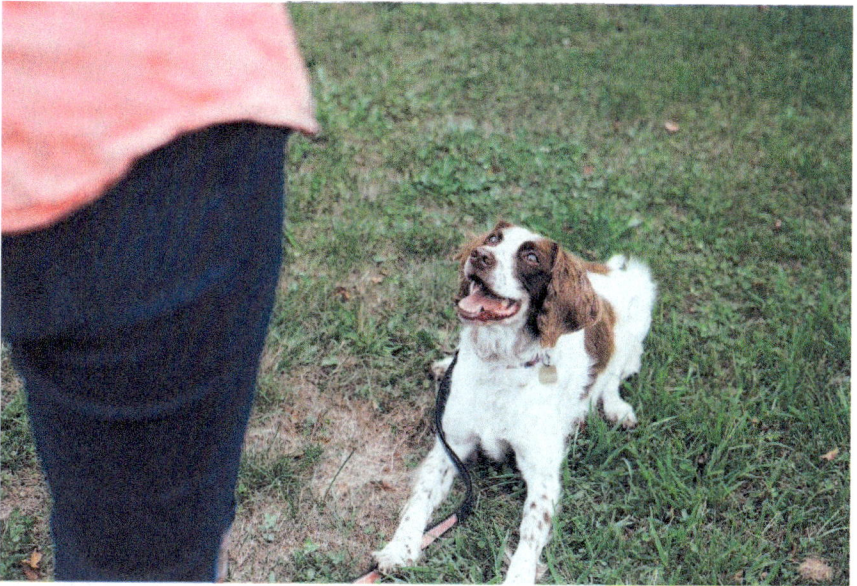

Start with the clicker and high-value treats at the ready.

1. Go to a quiet space for training with your pup.

2. Start the training process for laying down with the "sit" command. (If you need to, revisit the previous training section to be sure your dog is ready to move ahead to learn to lie down.) Click and reward the "sit".

3. With a treat in hand, use the command "down" or "lie down" and lower your hand with the treat to the ground. If they lie down, click and reward immediately.

4. If your pup doesn't lay down when the treat is moved to the ground with your hand, try moving it across the ground slightly to get their attention. This should motivate them to investigate what is happening down on the ground. When they lay down, click and reward immediately.

5. Continue repeating step five in increments until they follow the "down" command without moving the treat to the ground. Then repeat step four several times with an immediate click and reward as soon as their belly touches the floor.

6. Now, you can start adding some duration to the "down" by waiting a few seconds to click and reward once they're down. Gradually increase the time between when they lay down to when you click the clicker and reward the behavior.

7. Use a release phrase to let them know when it's okay to stand up or move out of the lying down position, like "okay" or "free." When they have mastered laying down for several moments, say the release phrase and click and reward as soon as they leave the position. It's important to practice, mark, and reward both the duration of a pose as well as the release individually so that they will eventually wait for the release in the future.

8. Go to a variety of different environments to practice "down" and release "free" or "okay" from the down position. Incorporating different environments into the training process after a command has been mastered tells your dog that the same behavior is expected from them regardless of their surroundings.

Stay

1. Gather the clicker and your pup's favorite treats for a 10-minute training session.

2. Ensure the environment is quiet and distraction-free.

3. Call your dog by name to get their attention.

4. Show them the clicker in your hand but do not click it just yet.

5. Be sure that your dog has mastered the "sit" and "down" commands as they form the basis for the "stay" command.

6. Begin by asking your dog to sit or lie down and follow up with a click of the clicker and treat.

7. While your dog is sitting or lying down, hold your hand palm out in front of you while facing your dog. This will help them pair a visual cue with the behavior you're asking from them.

8. Maintain eye contact, keep your hand extended, then take a step backward. If your dog stays sitting or lying down, immediately click the clicker and reward it with a treat. If they do not stay, go back to step six and try again.

9. Repeat step eight several times until your dog stays consistent every time you take a step back.

10. Add a verbal cue of "stay" as you take a step back and repeat step eight a few more times.

11. Start adding additional steps back gradually while clicking and rewarding with each progression.

12. When your dog has mastered staying in a sitting or lying down position while you've taken several steps away from them, start adding in something a little more challenging. Try walking to the side or turning your back to them for a moment while they're sitting. Always reward the "stay" directly after presenting the new challenge with a click and a treat.

13. When they have accomplished several variations of the "stay" you can introduce a release command. So, instead of clicking and rewarding to release them, use a cue such as "okay" or "free" while dropping your hand down, then click and reward when they get up out of their sitting or lying down position.

14. Repeat the stay command with variations, and release the stay with the click and reward. When you feel your pup has successfully learned the behaviors you're asking for, try practicing them in other environments. You may need to repeat

parts of this training process to remind your pup of what you're asking them to do, but they will learn that while the environment may change, the command and reward will stay consistent.

Come

1. Have the clicker ready.

2. Set aside a supply of treats.

3. Get a long leash to use for training.

4. Attach the leash to your dog's collar and allow it to drag behind them.

5. Get your dog's attention by calling their name while using a positive and encouraging tone of voice.

6. Say the cue "come" clearly and distinctly. The cue "come" can be replaced with "here" or "recall" if preferred, but once a cue is chosen, then it should remain consistent.

7. Encourage your dog to come to you by using the cue and clapping your hands or patting your thigh. As soon as they get to you, click the clicker and give them a treat. If necessary, you can use the leash to guide them to you gently.

8. Repeat the process several times and gradually decrease the encouragement with your hands. Continue to click and reward immediately. When they start coming when called reliably, you can remove the leash from their collar.

9. Start gradually increasing the time between when your dog gets to you and when you click and reward the expected behavior.

10. When they respond positively and consistently to the command, try challenging them with a new environment. Stay

consistent in the click and reward so they learn that the behavior also needs to remain consistent regardless of the environment.

Leave It

1. Have the clicker ready to go.

2. Prepare a supply of treats your pup loves.

3. Move to a quiet place without distractions and bring a bit of your dog's kibble (if you're not using that for their motivational treat, otherwise use a toy or bone).

4. With the bit of kibble in your hand, show it to your dog and, using a firm tone of voice, say, "Leave it." Do not give your dog the kibble in your hand.

5. Wait until your pup turns away or is distracted by something, and immediately click the clicker and reward with the training treat (not the kibble).

6. Show your pup your hand with the kibble, say "Leave it," wait for them to eventually turn away when you don't give it to them, click the clicker, and reward.

7. Repeat this process several times before progressing. Then, set the kibble on the ground and say, "Leave it." Click and reward immediately if they hesitate to get to the kibble.

8. Move the kibble to a different spot, say "leave it," click, and reward if they do not move the kibble.

9. Try making this exercise more challenging by using a favorite toy instead of kibble and repeating steps five through eight.

10. Take the exercise one step further by repeating the "leave it" command in several new environments. Mastering this exercise

can save your dog's life one day should they encounter something interesting or dangerous.

Off

1. Gather the clicker for a training session.

2. Supply yourself with some of their favorite treats.

3. Set a distraction by choosing a surface you want your dog to move away from, such as a couch or bed.

4. Stand close to the surface and use a firm voice to say "off." Point to the surface you want them to move away from as you say the cue.

5. Wait for your pup to make any motion away from the surface you're pointing to. This could be as little as lifting a paw or taking a step back. Immediately click and reward with a treat.

6. If your pup doesn't understand and isn't moving away from the surface you're pointing to, try placing a treat on the ground close to the surface but just out of reach. You may have to act quickly here, but say the command "off", click, and reward as soon as they move away from the surface.

7. If necessary, repeat step six several times before attempting the exercise without the treat on the ground. Then, repeat step five several times as well.

8. Once your pup has figured out what you're asking for, gradually increase the distance your dog needs to move away before you click and reward it with a treat.

9. When they're ready for a challenge, introduce a different surface and repeat the steps. You can use this command when you want them to step off of a rug you're trying to move, to get

out of the car when you arrive somewhere, or to get down from the furniture.

Stand

1. Gather the clicker.

2. Have treats ready for training.

3. Move to a quiet space where your pup won't be easily distracted.

4. Have your pup start in a lying-down position. (Revisit the "down" exercise if necessary.)

5. While your dog is calm and attentive, hold a treat in your hand at nose level and say "stand" while moving the treat upward. Click and reward the moment that your dog begins to rise with the treat.

6. Practice step five several times and gradually increase the standing time before you reward with a click and a treat.

7. Once the association has been made between the reward and the cue, practice starting from a sitting position as well. This will help reinforce that standing is standing regardless of the position they start in.

8. Try practicing this command from various environments to encourage the same behavior regardless of your surroundings.

Place (or Mat)

1. Prepare to train by having the clicker ready.

2. Gather treats for the training session.

3. Choose a specific area or mat to be the designated "place".

4. Show your dog the mat or area and give them treats for showing interest.

5. In an encouraging voice, say the cue "place" or "mat" (choose one cue or the other but do not interchange both).

6. Motion to the mat while saying the cue.

7. Immediately click and reward any step on or toward the mat.

8. Return their attention to the mat, say the cue, click, and reward with a treat.

9. Repeat step eight until a clear association between the behavior and reward has been identified by your pup.

10. Create a more challenging scenario by incorporating other training commands into this process, such as "come" and then returning to the mat with "place." Or, once they're complying with "place," ask them to sit or lie down. Click and reward with each successfully achieved compliance. This exercise is great when smaller kids visit and your dog gets a little overexcited. They can go to their place and greet visitors from there until they've calmed down a bit.

Touch (or Target)

1. Begin the exercise with the clicker in hand.

2. Be sure to have a stash of treats at the ready.

3. Choose a target object such as a stick or a toy.

4. Bring the target object to their nose, say "target," and click the clicker and reward with a treat when they inch forward to investigate.

5. Repeat step four several times. After associating with the reward and behavior, try using the cue without bringing the target to their nose. When they approach the target, click and reward.

6. Repeat step five several times. Once they are consistently coming to the target when cued, try placing the target on the ground. Cue the command while pointing at the target. Click and reward any approach to the target.

7. With the target on the ground, gradually hold out on the click and reward until they come closer and closer to the target, consistently pointing and cueing the command. The goal is that they will eventually come to the target for a nose touch when asked.

8. Click and reward several successful "touch" commands, and then swap out the target for something new. If necessary, repeat steps in this process to show them that the expectation is the same regardless of the target.

9. When they've mastered all the steps up to this point for "target," take a basket of different items to different locations and practice with various items. If you want to take this command to the next level, try placing a plethora of items on the ground, all spaced out. Point and cue different items with each command. Reward them when they touch the one you pointed to.

Back (or Back up)

1. Have your clicker at the ready.

2. Gather your pup's favorite treats.

3. Go to a quiet and distraction-free area.

4. Your dog can begin in either a sitting or standing position.

5. Holding a treat in your hand, at your pup's nose level, say "back" or "back up" in a firm but non-aggressive tone.

6. Move the treat toward your pup's chest, encouraging them to take a step back. The moment they take a step backward, click and reward them with the treat.

7. Repeat step six several times, then gradually ask for more distance when backing up before rewarding with a click and treat.

8. Phase out by motioning the treat toward their chest and relying on the cue and click to indicate the action you're looking for.

9. You can level this command by adding a "sit" or "stay" at the end. Always click and reward after they complete the ask.

These basic clicker training commands are crucial for contributing to a well-behaved and well-adjusted canine companion. They provide the foundation of communication between the pet and the owner. They feed the confidence of the pets and owners, ultimately keeping everyone safe and happy. They also allow enjoying outings in public as well as promote a calmer and easier day-to-day life at home. With expectations communicated, we can prevent problem behaviors and increase the quality of life for the whole family (including your fur baby).

Chapter 5:

Problem-Solving and Behavior

Modification Using a Clicker

What are some common behavioral issues, and why do they occur? These questions are important to understand before proceeding in trying to fix them. Ideally, the clicker training program would begin before these issues arise and likely be prevented altogether. However, if you're a dog owner who has only recently come across our training guide and these behaviors have already begun, that's okay! We're here for you!

Dealing with Common Behavior Issues

Destructive Chewing

- **Why?** - Dogs chew for various reasons, but the most common tend to be because of boredom, teething in puppies, anxiety, hunger, pent-up energy, etc. Some dogs chew to explore their environment, play, or get your attention. After all, negative attention is still attention, right? This can be incredibly frustrating if their chewing is damaging furniture, clothes, shoes, and plants. Not only is it frustrating, but it is also expensive and potentially dangerous. Dogs that chew inedible things are at risk of fracturing their teeth, cutting their gums, or getting intestinal blockages that need surgical removal.

- **Prevention** - I'm not sure there's a cure-all for puppies that are chewing. However, you can help prevent them from chewing your favorite shoes or rug. For starters, limit access to valuables when your pup is not in direct supervision. Shoes must be behind closed doors, toys put into toy boxes with lids, and trash bins must have a locking lid or be put into a cabinet. Also, make sure your pup has options that are okay to chew. Depending on the type of chewer they are, a heavy-duty rubber toy, rawhides, or other veterinarian-approved toy should always be available, especially when your pup isn't being directly supervised.

Training -

1. Gather the clicker and your pup's treats of choice.

2. Have several toys available that your dog is allowed to chew.

3. This is the tricky part. When you catch your dog chewing something they shouldn't, calmly replace it with an appropriate chew toy. When they show interest in the more appropriate chew toy, click and reward them with a treat.

4. Be consistent in repeating step three, as timing is crucial for them to make the connection between the correct chew toy and the reward they're being given.

5. After several successful chew toy replacements, begin using a cue to associate with the correct toy for them to chew, such as "chew" or "toy". They will gradually associate the cue with the appropriate behavior you're asking for and be discouraged from chewing anything else.

6. To elevate the training here, place several things they would normally be tempted to chew alongside sometimes they are allowed to chew. Then, use the cue you've chosen, "toy" or "chew," and click and reward the correct choice in a chew toy.

Digging

- **Why?** - There are tons of reasons why dogs dig. So many it's odd when a dog doesn't go through a digging phase at all. Some breeds are genetically inclined to dig for hunting or to bury things. Other dogs might find that they can get to a new area to explore or escape if they dig. Dogs also dig shallow pits for a cooler surface to lie on. If there is a new scent in the garden, they might dig to uncover what it might be. And some dogs will even dig to alleviate stress or anxiety. Whatever the reason, it isn't ideal for the owner in most cases. Digging can also lead to injuries for your dog, depending on the material being dug into.

- **Prevention** - Supervision is the best way to prevent a dog from digging. If it seems that they are digging regularly and you're not sure of the reason, consult a vet to resolve any potential medical conditions that might be causing the behavior. Beat boredom by playing with your dog, providing toys, and taking them out regularly for exercise.

Training -

1. Gather the clicker and high-value treats for opportunistic training.

2. Identify an area where they can dig harmlessly.

3. If they start to dig somewhere, they shouldn't redirect them (with a leash if necessary) to the area they are allowed to dig. Click and reward when their attention goes toward the digging area.

4. If necessary, entice them to dig in the new area by burying some treats.

5. Identify a cue to use, such as "dig," and time the cue when they begin showing interest in the buried treats. Click and reward any attention toward the buried treats, such as pawing or sniffing the ground.

6. Redirect gently and use the clicker with treats at every opportunity toward interest or digging in the designated area. It's a fun game to return to occasionally and replace hidden treats for your pup. It will encourage them to keep coming back to check out what's new in the digging area next time they're bored.

Jumping

- **Why?** - Jumping is a natural dog behavior that often starts in puppyhood and only increases when people react and give attention, even unintentionally, to the behavior. Dogs will jump when they are excited to interact socially with humans and other dogs. This is normally a playful behavior but can turn into an indication of dominance. The best thing to do is begin deterring and training the behavior out of your dog as early as possible.

- **Prevention** - As hard as it may seem, try only to give your attention to your dog when they have four paws on the ground. It may mean ignoring them for a moment until they get curious enough to stop jumping, but giving them attention when they jump up only rewards the unwanted behavior. Also, excess energy can result in more jumping. Be sure to exercise your dog regularly, as this will help them jump less.

Training -

1. With the clicker and their favorite treats in hand, approach a common situation where they are likely to jump.

2. When the situation arises, such as someone comes to visit, instruct the person not to give your pup any attention initially.

3. As soon as all four paws are on the ground (you may have to be very quick!), click the clicker and reward with a treat.

4. A cue such as "feet" (if the cue "down" is already being used to get off of furniture) can be used to associate with all feet being on the ground. Use the cue the moment all four feet are grounded, click, and reward immediately.

5. It may help to use a training cue that your pup has already mastered.", such as "sit." Even if they have fully mastered "sit," it is important to click and reward every opportunity where your pup has chosen the trained behavior over jumping.

Pulling on a Leash

- **Why?** - Going for a walk will excite your pup! They see walks as an adventure and are eager to see what lies behind every corner. On walks, so many new sites, sounds, and smells exist to investigate. If you encounter new people or dogs, the excitement can increase exponentially. They will want to get to where they're going as quickly as possible to avoid missing out on something. Unfortunately, this excitement often leads to pulling on a leash. While your dog pulling you around can be fairly annoying, another reason to nip it in the bud is that it can also be hazardous. Imagine trying to navigate walking down a set of stairs with your dog pulling you along. Or, if they suddenly spot a new pup across the street while a car is driving down the road...the dangerous scenarios are endless.

- **Prevention** - Exercising your dog before putting them on a leash for a walk can help diminish their energy and reduce pulling.

Another technique to stop pulling is to stop walking every time the pulling begins. Your pup may associate pulling with a lack of forward movement.

Training -

1. With the clicker and preferred treats at the ready, attach your pup's leash to their collar.

2. Begin walking, and while the leash is still loose, click and give a treat to reward walking with a loose leash.

3. If they start to pull, stop walking, wait for them to come to you, and let slack into the leash. Click and reward the loose leash immediately.

4. Repeat steps two and three several times, even if it means making very little progress forward. The key is to be consistent. Pulling will immediately stop forward movement, the loose leash will be rewarded, and movement will continue.

5. If you haven't already, consider getting a harness for your dog that allows the leash to clip in the front. This will create a force that will redirect your dog's attention back to you when they pull.

6. Introduce a cue such as "heel" to indicate your dog should come back to you. Use the cue after they've started pulling, you've stopped the forward movement, and they've returned to you where you're standing to investigate. Click and reward them every time they come back to stand at your side.

7. Repeat several short leash training sessions with your pup while maintaining consistency and positivity. They'll pick up what you're asking for when the message is clear and concise every time.

House Soiling

- **Why?** - If your dog is not a young puppy and still soiling in the house, have them evaluated by a veterinarian to rule out any medical conditions that could be causing them to relieve themselves indoors. If they've been given the "all-clear" by your vet, then there could be other reasons why they're still soiling the house. Some reasons a dog might "go" in the house are for territorial purposes, overexcitement, a change in environment or routine, a lack of access to the yard, or simply incomplete house training.

- **Prevention** - The best prevention we can recommend is ensuring your dog has ample access to go outside. Also, ensure the designated potty area is free from clutter and debris and regularly cleared of their excrement. If your dog has an accident in the house, clean the area thoroughly and remove any scent that could encourage repeat offenses. Refrain from feeding your pup too close to bedtime, and do not leave them without access to outside and without supervision for long periods.

Training -

1. Have the clicker and preferred treats at the ready.

2. Decide where you would prefer your dog to do their business.

3. Use a leash when you take them outside so that they can only explore the "potty area."

4. Take note of when they eat and drink and keep their feeding schedule consistent.

5. After they've eaten, take them outside to the potty area repeatedly until they eventually *go*. Be patient, as this could take several tries. The trick is to give them ample opportunity to *go* in the designated area and very little opportunity to *go* anywhere else. Click and reward them the second they finish going. It is important not to interrupt them mid-process!

6. Repeat step five after meals and every two hours throughout the day.

7. Introduce a cue such as "go potty" that is used in the training process as they start to *go*.

8. Start taking your dog outside to potty without the leash. Click and reward them when they follow you to the potty area via a "come" command. Click and reward again when they also follow the "go potty" cue.

9. You can eventually increase the durations between potty breaks, but be sure they are still regularly let outside to the designated potty area several times a day.

If there is a regression in potty training (they wouldn't be the first dog this happened to), take a step or two back in this process and spend a few more days focused on training. Some dogs will pick it up more quickly than others, but they will eventually achieve potty training success with consistency.

Fear and Anxiety in Dogs

Barking

Excessive and/or aggressive barking in dogs can be due to several factors. Some dogs will bark more when they have excess energy as a way of expressing themselves. Some will use barking as a tool to indicate what they perceive as a threat. If a dog is unfamiliar with a sound, a new person, or other dogs, they may bark out of anxiety. Dogs that haven't been properly socialized or trained might lack confidence, leading to excessive or aggressive barking. With clicker training, there are steps that you can take to help your dog understand that barking is not always necessary.

1. Have the clicker and treats ready.

2. Take note of triggers that instigate barking for your dog.

3. Decide on a verbal cue such as "quiet" or "enough."

4. When the trigger occurs, wait for a moment of pause in your dog's barking, then click and reward immediately.

5. Use the verbal cue the moment your dog allows for a quiet moment, then click and reward them for that moment.

6. Repeat steps four or five several times until you feel incredible your dog has made the association between the desired behavior and the reward.

Correcting this behavior takes incredible patience and perfect timing but can result in a more confident dog and a more enjoyable relationship. When necessary, incorporate a leash to maintain your dog's focus on the training. Gradually challenge your dog with new and exciting experiences while maintaining the routine and consistency of the clicker training for "quiet". They'll catch on quicker than you might think!

Separation Anxiety

Dogs may express their separation anxiety in a variety of ways. Some dogs will try to escape their enclosure when you leave. Other dogs will bark excessively and seemingly at nothing when you're gone. Others might regress to soiling in the house or start expressing destructive behaviors such as chewing on furniture or other non-chewables in the house.

You can help your dog through these difficult and overwhelming feelings by providing them with a safe space they are accustomed to and containing safe and familiar items. Also, exercising your dog regularly will help them stay calm when you're not there.

1. Start with shorter durations of leaving them alone so they get used to what it feels like without panicking.

2. Upon return, click and reward them when they haven't expressed any destructive behaviors.

3. Avoiding excessive attention to destructive behaviors or greeting them overly enthusiastic when leaving and returning will help. Maintaining a calm and soothing presence when leaving and returning will help show them that there is nothing to get too excited about.

4. Gradually increase the duration of time they're left alone and use the clicker and treats upon each return.

5. Mimic the motions of getting ready to leave and use the clicker and reward system when they exhibit calm behavior.

If your dog continues to display separation anxiety after several attempts at training them, consult a physician for potential behavior modification assistance.

Phobias (General, Social, or Specific Phobias)

Dogs have phobias much in the same way that humans do. They are often expressed as pacing, panting, shaking or trembling, hiding, excessive drooling, and is aggressive when aggressive or destructive behaviors. Use clicker training to help counter-condition them to the stimulus that is causing the fear positively and gently.

1. Please take note of what is causing their phobia. This could be other dogs, new people, or several other triggers.

2. Also, take safety measures when working with a scared dog. If necessary, consult a professional if your dog is aggressive when scared.

3. Have a clicker and several treats ready to work with.

4. Start small with minimal exposure to the stimulus.

5. Stay calm and have a positive tone when introducing the phobia trigger.

6. Keep a safe distance from the trigger initially, then close the gap as they become more comfortable.

7. Click and reward any sign of calmness or curiosity. This could look like a bit of a tail wag, sniffing in the direction of the stimulant, or just a pause in barking.

8. In this scenario, training sessions can be much shorter than 10 minutes. Starting with very short and positive exposures will make the most improvement.

9. As your dog becomes more accustomed to being exposed to their phobia, increase exposure timeframes or intensity.

10. Continue regular training sessions so that their phobia does not redevelop.

Compulsives (Tail Chasing, Excessive Licking, or Pacing)

Some breeds of dogs are more prone to compulsive behaviors than others. Some compulsions include excessive licking, tail chasing, pacing or circling, digging, and self-mutilation. It is important to take note of these behaviors as soon as possible as they can become destructive and harmful to your dog. Always consult a veterinarian if your dog is displaying compulsive behaviors that are causing physical harm.

Compulsive behaviors tend to be less drastic when a dog is being regularly exercised and has had proper training. If both of these boxes are "checked" with your dog and they still exhibit compulsive behavior, you can try taking these steps with clicker training.

1. Gather the clicker and some treats. Have them accessible at opportunistic moments.

2. When your dog begins exhibiting compulsive behavior, use a distraction to get them to stop, such as bringing out a toy or using a training cue previously learned.

3. Click and reward your dog the moment that they stop the compulsive behavior.

4. Regularly repeat the distraction, click, and reward each time they begin the compulsive behavior. It will take time, timing, and consistency, but the behavior should lessen considerably if not entirely.

Aggression and Reactivity

Excessive Excitability

Excessive excitability can be displayed in dogs via impulse behaviors described previously, excessive barking, jumping, or mouthing (this is when they bite without any force that harms), they can be restless, or they might dart off when reacting to stimuli. Regular exercise and mental stimulation (training and new toys) can sometimes help with these behaviors. If you've completed the basic training steps contained in this book and exercise your dog regularly, then continued displays of excessive excitability may need to be discussed with your veterinarian.

Territorial Aggression

Territorial aggression often presents as barking or growling at perceived intruders, lunging or charging aggressively at other humans or animals, taking a protective stance with their hackles raised (like a mohawk down their spine), biting or nipping, and persistent boundary defense (constantly looking out for a threat). Training and socializing a dog should lessen these behaviors. Seek professional training or guidance should your dog continue displaying these behaviors after several attempts of clicker training, regular exercise, and socialization sessions.

Possessive Aggression

Possessive aggression in dogs can be very dangerous and should be addressed by a professional. Signs of possessive aggression include growling or snarling when someone approaches their possession, biting or snapping at someone when they try to take something away, raised hackles or stiff body language, guarding or hovering near food, gulping food down quickly, or stiffening their body stance when anyone gets near them while they have something (this often includes food). Some clicker training techniques, such as the "leave it" command with a click and reward, can be used here. This can desensitize them enough to realize that giving up what they have might result in a reward or something even better. Be cautious with training and ensure professional advice is adhered to in order to avoid injury.

Chapter 6:

Advanced Training Using a Clicker

Advanced clicker training takes the basics of clicker training to the next level. Before venturing into this chapter, ensure you and your pup have successfully mastered all the basic training exercises. Indeed, every basic exercise is not required to move on to advanced clicker training, but by going through the process of learning all of the basics with your pup, you're setting them up to become eager and expert-level clicker training learners. With the training foundation that the basic exercises lay, your pup has come to interpret the clicker as a clear and consistent signal that they have performed the desired behaviors that you're looking for. They have been consistently rewarded for their efforts. Setting that learning foundation will have your pup looking for the right answer in the advanced training exercises to come in this chapter.

We'll use techniques in this chapter such as shaping, target training by direction, and then chaining or combining, simple behaviors to get the desired result. Shaping is the process of training a series of small steps to be combined later into one fluid behavior. It allows the dog to break down the task into bite-sized pieces and then assemble the puzzle slowly until it can be performed as a whole. Target training involves directing a dog to a particular location and asking them to perform the behavior once they're there. With target training, there are a series of steps to condition a dog into moving in the correct direction until they've reached the target. The steps are repeated until the dog can associate the location with the commands. Chaining is the process in which multiple behaviors are combined to obtain an understanding of a complex exercise. While the separate behaviors can be taught in any order, once they are chained together, the reward only comes after completing the final behavior. This fixes the set chain in a particular order so that it can be performed again and again with the same desired outcome.

For the exercises to come, being that all the basic training exercises are to have been thoroughly trained beforehand, we'll leave out the reminders to have your clicker and treats at the ready. By now, you and your pup are experts in the training setup process and know how to prepare before training. We have added to each advanced training exercise the prerequisite basic training commands that will be essential in your pup learning the more complicated behaviors listed in this chapter. Be sure that the prerequisite training commands are reinforced before starting the new exercise.

Teaching Tricks

Play Dead with a Bang

1. Prerequisite - Down or Lie Down

2. You'll want to start this trick training with your pup in the lying-down position.

3. Most dogs will stay upright in the lying-down position, but you'll want them to take it one step further by laying their body to one side with their head resting on the ground. With a treat in hand, bring the treat to your dog's nose and then move it slowly to the ground on one side or the other. It is likely your dog will have a preferred side to lie on, so take your time finding which side they prefer.

4. As soon as they start to roll their shoulder into a lying-down position, click and reward them with a treat.

5. Repeat the lie-down motion several times and add the verbal cue "bang".

6. Once your dog has associated the reward with the cue and behavior, repeat the exercise several more times, adding a gun-like hand signal.

7. Gradually move the treat further from their nose and with less motion toward the ground until they lie their entire body, including their head, on the ground. Click and reward their efforts immediately.

8. After repeating step seven several times, remove any and motion with a treat entirely. Use only the verbal cue and hand motion to indicate the asked behavior. Click and reward immediately.

9. Once your pup has gotten comfortable with going from the lying down position to being rolled over to one side with their head on the ground using only the verbal and hand motion cues, try having them start from a sitting position to perform the same action. If necessary, you can use a treat in hand motioning to the ground to help them understand that you're asking for the same behavior regardless of the position they start in.

10. You can begin challenging your dog further by cueing the Play Dead with a Bang exercise from a standing position, taking them to different environments with various distractions, and practicing step nine several more times. Remember to limit training sessions to 10 minutes. If you don't get through all of the steps for this exercise, that's okay! Start a step or two before where you ended with your last session and build on what they've learned in the next. This exercise could likely take several training sessions before mastering it entirely.

Fetch Specific Items by Name

1. Start this exercise with one particular toy or item your dog is interested in. With training sessions limited to 10 minutes, only train one item at a time for the first few sessions. Once your pup has learned to fetch a few specific items by name, you can combine their commands into the same training session. We'll explain more in the steps to come.

2. With the item of choice at the ready, decide the cue for that item. Make sure to stay consistent with the names of each item you train with your dog so as not to confuse them.

3. Offer the item to your dog, and when they take it, use the cue or name for it along with a click and then reward with a treat.

4. Repeat step three several times until your dog understands ,they are being rewarded for taking the item. Then, begin setting the item in front of them and use the same cue to indicate that you want them to pick it up. Click and reward them with a treat when they pick up the item. If they don't understand what you're asking, go back to step three for a bit more practice.

5. Once your dog reliably picks the item up on cue and with the verbal command, start gradually placing it further away from them and practicing the same exercise from various distances. If you feel they've gotten the hang of this, move on to step 6.

6. Place the item on the ground and then walk out of the room. The item should be just out of site. Use the verbal cue for that item and click and reward the retrieval.

7. Choose three items that you'll practice these steps with. On the fourth training session, bring two of the items together to train with. Follow the same steps but with the items placed side by side. If necessary, repeat steps three and four repeatedly for each item. Graduate to placing both items on the ground and cueing for one and then the other. Click and reward for each successful choice of item.

8. When they're ready, introduce the third item and practice the exercises again. They've mastered this exercise when they can successfully retrieve the correct item from a location out of sight and among other available items.

Rollover

1. Prerequisite - Down or Lie Down

2. If your pup has mastered the playing dead trick, rolling over might come more easily to them. Start them in the lying down position.

3. Use a treat in hand to slowly motion from their nose, over one of their shoulders, and down to the ground. Move very slowly so that they can follow the motion with their nose, and, ultimately, with their body. Click and reward when they get their head to the floor.

4. With their head on the floor and another treat in hand, bring the treat to their nose and slowly motion over their shoulder and toward the ground behind their back. Again, move slowly here so that their only option for getting the treat is to follow your hand and roll their body to the other side. Be patient, as this can take several attempts before they understand what you're asking.

5. If necessary, click and reward any small movement in the right direction when moving the treat over their shoulder. Gradually increase the amount of movement you require before rewarding them with a click and a treat.

6. Practice steps four or five until they complete the rollover with the click and reward. Then, add the verbal cue "rollover" just as their legs come over their body in the motion. Click and reward the success several times.

7. Make this trick a bit more challenging by introducing a rollover in the opposite direction. When they've mastered a rollover in each direction, start practicing these tricks interchangeably. This will solidify the exercise.

Ring a Doorbell or Alarm

1. Prerequisite - Touch

2. Purchase a mobile bell or alarm before beginning this training exercise. Several can be mounted to a door or wall after training has been mastered.

3. Place the bell or alarm close to your dog's nose and use the command "touch". If they mastered "touch" from the basic

training exercises, they will likely comply readily. Click and reward the touch from their nose.

4. Place the alarm or bell on the ground in front of them and use the "touch" command. Click and reward with a treat.

5. Practice with the bell or alarm nearby several times and follow up with a click and a treat. Then, gradually begin placing the bell or alarm further away from your dog. Click and reward them when they successfully ring it.

6. Elevate this training practice by mounting the bell or alarm close to the door they would use to go outside. Each time you let them out to go potty, have them touch the alarm and then follow up with a click and reward. It may take a week or two, but eventually, they will be conditioned to ring the bell or alarm when they want to go outside to potty. That's right - no more guesswork for when they need to *go*!

Limbo Under an Object

1. Prerequisite - Down or Lie Down

2. Start your dog in the down position and get into a position low to the ground close in front of them, such as on hands and knees.

3. Use one hand with the palm facing up and fingers together facing toward your dog. Motion to them by curling your fingers inward two or three times. If they inch toward you or stretch their neck forward, click and reward them with a treat.

4. Repeat step three several times until there is a consistent forward-type motion when the hand movement is used. Then, move slightly back and away from your pup and repeat the exercise.

5. Gradually move backward further and further with each practice until they are crawling several steps to you before clicking and rewarding them.

6. When they've mastered a crawl, begin using a hidden object, such as a broomstick suspended between two chairs for them to crawl under. Initially, be sure they have plenty of head clearance so they become comfortable with the behavior you're asking of them. Click and reward them after they successfully crawl under the object.

7. Increase the challenge of this exercise by changing out the objects that you're asking them to crawl under. Then, gradually decrease the amount of headspace they have going under the object. Your pup is sure to impress you with how low they can go!

Advanced Obedience

Extended-Duration Commands

Extended-duration commands involve teaching your dog to hold a desired position or behavior for several seconds before they receive the click and reward, telling them they've completed it successfully. This is useful for times when you need your dog to hold a cue without immediately snapping back out of it. Certain situations might include the scenario described earlier in this book where a ball rolls into the road. You may need your dog to sit and stay for several seconds while you retrieve the ball safely and without them following you into the road. Ideally, your dog would be able to hold any pose or command for an extended period until they are given a signal from you to release the pose. We'll cover a general set of guidelines to teach an extended-duration command that can be used with any of the commands contained in this book thus far.

1. Start with one of the basic commands, such as "sit."

2. Repeat the basic training steps for "sit" several times with the click and treat for reward.

3. Gradually increase the time between when they comply with the command, and you click and reward them with a treat. You will be able to increase the time they wait for the click significantly by reinforcing the behavior consistently every time.

4. Start to incorporate a release word such as "okay" to let them know when they can move out of the initial command. Give a click and a treat as they move out with the release cue.

5. Practice step four consistently and continue to increase the time they must wait to be released. If they come out of the pose early, do not scold them. Simply command them back to the "sit" and reduce the amount of time they need to wait for the click and reward. Then you can begin increasing the duration they must wait again.

6. To increase the difficulty level here, try asking them to "sit" and then turn your back on them for a moment. Say the release cue, and click and reward them with a treat. As they can wait longer in the stance, you can incorporate a new level of difficulty by moving around the room or even walking out of sight while they wait for the release cue. With every increase in difficulty, be sure to practice several times with immediate clicks and rewards each time they accomplish the intended behavior.

Heel Off Leash

1. Before starting this exercise, be sure that you're in a safely enclosed area with your dog with minimal distractions.

2. Your dog will naturally follow you, but the trick here is to associate the position of them coming to your side with the command "heel". First, have a treat in hand and let them sniff it without allowing them to take it.

3. Start to take a few steps away from them with the hand holding the treat at your side. When they begin following you, say "heel," then click and reward them with the treat.

4. Practice step three several times while only moving away short distances. As they become consistent with coming to your side, quicken your pace when you move away. Say "heel" and click and reward when they come to your side.

5. Try to increase the difficulty of this exercise by turning away from them, pretending to be interested in something else, then using the command, click, and reward when they come to your side.

6. Once you're confident in the yard that your dog has associated the "heel" command with coming to your side, start practicing in other environments. You can use areas of your house take them out on a long leash for a walk and continue practicing steps four and five.

7. Eventually, with consistency in the clicker training steps mentioned thus far, you will be able to go out in public areas (where dogs are allowed off-lease, of course) and continue practicing the heel off-leash. This exercise will become stronger and stronger the more it is practiced with increasing levels of distraction.

Stand and Stay

1. Prerequisites - Stand and Stay

2. This exercise will chain together two commands your dog has mastered from the Basic Obedience Commands chapter (Chapter Four). Give your dog the "stand" command, click the clicker, and reward them with a treat when they comply.

3. While they are standing, and directly after you've rewarded them for it, use the "stay" command. Wait just a moment and then follow up with a click and reward.

4. Repeat step three several times. Once they are regularly complying with staying a moment in the standing position,

gradually increase the amount of time before you click the clicker and reward them.

5. Once they are waiting nicely for several moments in the stand position, begin using a release word like "okay" to let them know when they can break out of the position. Always click and reward them with a treat when they leave the command position.

6. Increase the difficulty level in this exercise by removing the click and reward from the "stand" cue. Instead, use the "stand" cue and immediately follow it up with "stay". Wait a moment while they comply before clicking and rewarding them with a treat.

7. With the command chain in practice, begin increasing the duration you're asking them to stand again. You can also increase the difficulty with this command chain by walking away from them before you release, click, and reward them.

Agility and Dog Sports

Agility Course

Turn Left and Right

1. Pre-requisite - Sit, Stay, and Heel

2. Start with your dog in a standing position. Use a treat to lure your dog to one side or the other while saying the associated cue, such as "left" or "right". Click and reward them several times, going to one side, and then do the same on the other.

3. Start walking and ask your dog to "heel." Then turn in one direction or the other while saying the associated command of "left" or "right." Click and reward them for following you when you change direction.

4. Practice step three several times before introducing props. Once they comply consistently, you can use cones to increase their understanding of what you're asking them to do. Have them sit and stay.

5. Walk a few paces away and put a treat under one of the cones. Say the cue "left" or "right" associated with the appropriate cone with the treat under it. When they touch the cone with their nose, click and reward them with a treat.

6. Practice step five on both sides several times until you can interchange the commands, and they go to the correct cone consistently. Be sure to click and reward each time they accomplish the task.

7. As they become comfortable with these commands, you can increase complexity by creating an obstacle course with cones. Walk through the cones indicating right and left turns slowly at first. Click and reward them on each of the turns.

8. Gradually move faster through the obstacle course with your dog and remove the clicks and rewards while maneuvering. When you exit the cones, click and reward them.

Weave Through Poles

1. Once they are moving through cones comfortably, as in the previous exercise, begin placing the cones closer together. Your pup will need to make tighter and tighter turns through the cones gradually. Click and reward each time they maneuver them successfully.

2. With the added difficulty in moving through closely aligned cones, swap the cones out for poles. If necessary, initially place the poles slightly further apart than the cones. Click and reward your dog for moving through the poles like they did with the cones.

3. For advanced weaving through poles, start placing the poles closer and closer together. Click and reward the instant they emerge from the poles on the other side. This will instigate some speed as they will want to get to the treat as fast as possible.

Navigate Tunnels

1. Prerequisites - Sit, Stay, Come

2. Start by introducing your dog to the tunnel. Let them see and sniff it without any commands or other expectations. Click and reward when they approach the tunnel or show interest.

3. Set up a short and straight tunnel to begin the training session with.

4. Have them sit and stay at one end of the tunnel.

5. Go to the other end of the tunnel and get low to the ground so your dog can see you through the opening.

6. Use the "come" command and pat the floor of the tunnel to help them understand it is safe to walk on. If necessary, you can toss a treat into the tunnel to encourage them to go in after it. Click and reward them for coming through the tunnel.

7. Once they go through the tunnel the first time, they will more readily go through it again. Repeat step six several times but without putting any treats in the tunnel. Click and reward each successful trip through the tunnel.

8. Start creating more of a challenge in this exercise by elongating the tunnel and several turns to navigate. It will soon become a fun game for them to play. Be sure to click and reward their inquisitive efforts.

Spin and Jump Through a Hoop

1. This trick will incorporate several steps and commands into one. Start with identifying cues that you will use for your dog to spin to the left or the right. For example, you can use "spin" to indicate they should go to the left and "twirl" to indicate that they should go to the right. Regardless of what you choose, be sure to stay consistent when you use them so your dog doesn't get confused.

2. With a treat in hand, hold it at nose level and slowly move it toward your dog's tail. As they follow it, keep it going around in a circle until they are facing you again. Click and reward with a treat.

3. Repeat step two several times and then do the same thing in the other direction.

4. Start incorporating the appropriate verbal cues as they are turning, and then gradually use the cue earlier and earlier until you are saying it just before they turn. Continue to click and reward for each turn.

5. Repeat step four several times in both directions, but stop using a treat in hand to lure them. Gradually make smaller and smaller hand motions until they are comfortably turning with only the verbal cue. Click and reward each turn.

6. You'll train the hoop jump separately now and incorporate the spin later. Start the hoop training by placing the hoop vertically but touching the ground between you and your dog.

7. Squat down so that you're looking at your dog through the hoop.

8. With a treat in hand, ask your dog to come. If necessary, put your hand holding the hoop through the hoop and lure them through. Click and reward them for stepping through.

9. Repeat step eight several times, but stop using a treat in hand to lure them, and gradually stand up with each completion so that

you no longer have to be squatted down when they come through the hoop. Click and reward each time they go through successfully.

10. When they are comfortable coming through the hoop by stepping over it on the ground, raise it by a few inches, and use a cue such as "jump" or "go" for the same behavior. They should still be able to step over the hoop comfortably. Click and reward them each time.

11. Repeat step ten several times, but gradually raise the hoop off of the ground until they have to jump to come through. Click and reward each jump-through.

12. To combine these steps, use a turning cue with a click and reward, then follow up immediately with a jump through the hoop with a click and reward.

13. Repeat step twelve in succession several times and then stop the click and reward after the spin. Instead, lead them straight into the jump through the hoop with the appropriate cue and only use the clicker and reward at the end of the series.

14. Repeat step thirteen several times using only verbal cues and a click and reward at the end of the spin and jump through the hoop.

Dance on Hind Legs

1. Decide what cue you want to use for your dog to stand on their hind legs, such as "up".

2. With a treat in hand, bring it to their nose level and then slowly raise it upward and slightly over their back. As their head moves up with the treat, click and reward them.

3. Repeat step two several times but gradually raise the treat higher each time until their front paws have to come off the ground a bit to get the treat. Click and reward immediately.

4. Start incorporating the verbal cue into the exercise as they bring their paws off the ground. Click and reward their efforts.

5. Repeat step four several times and then slowly begin raising the treat higher and higher until they are fully up on their hind legs when you click and reward them.

6. Gradually increase the time you require them to be on their hind legs before clicking and rewarding them for the right behavior. It may take some practice for them to balance this step, so be patient and practice often.

7. As they gain better balance on their hind legs, you can use the hand holding the treat to have them walk a pace or two or begin to turn a circle. Always go slow and reward baby steps as you go along with a click and a treat.

Chapter 7:

Understanding Dog Behavior

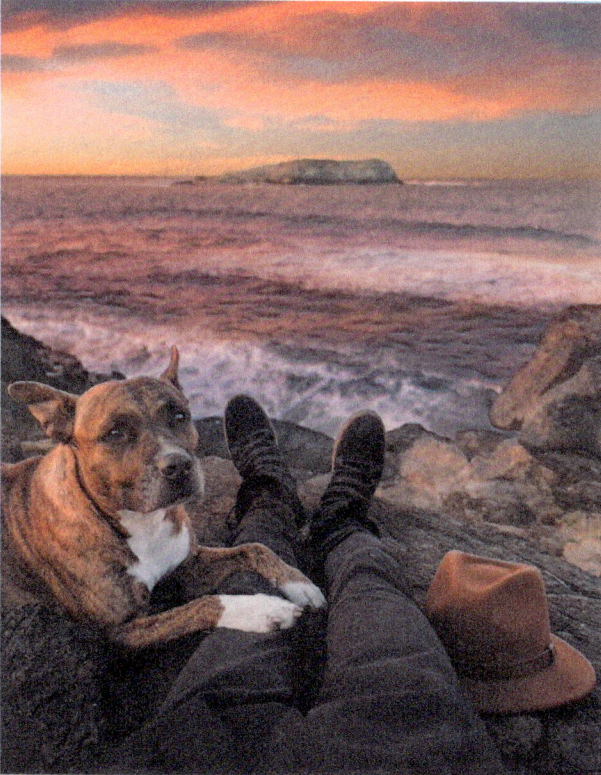

Why is It Important to Understand Dog Behaviors?

Understanding dog behavior is crucial for several reasons. For instance, they significantly promote a healthy relationship between the dog and their owner. Dogs communicate primarily through body language, vocalizations, and behavior. Understanding these cues allows for effective communication, fosters a stronger bond, and prevents misunderstandings. Misinterpreting a dog's behavior can lead to potentially unsafe situations. Knowing the difference between signs of fear, playfulness, or aggression is essential for responding appropriately.

Effective training relies on understanding canine behavior. Knowing how dogs learn, what motivates them, and how they respond to commands enhances the training process, leading to better obedience and desired behaviors. Being able to identify normal dog behavior helps to address potential behavioral issues before they escalate. Proactive measures can be taken throughout the training process to prevent issues such as aggression, anxiety, or destructive behaviors.

Recognizing and responding to a dog's needs contributes to a stronger bond and a trusting relationship between the owner and canine. Recognizing signs of discomfort, fear, or aggression can help prevent injuries or attacks when encountering new environments or unfamiliar dogs. You can count on your dog to tell you through their body language or behavior that they are not having a good time and make the appropriate adjustments to build their trust and confidence in your leadership.

By understanding your dog's behaviors, you can meet their basic needs, including proper nutrition, exercise, mental stimulation, and social interactions. It will contribute to better overall health and well-being for your dog. By knowing what behaviors are normal, you will be able to identify changes in their behavior and uncover potential health issues earlier. This can lead to earlier veterinary care and could potentially save their life.

You'll be able to identify potentially stressful environments or stimuli for your dog and make appropriate adjustments at home to create a soothing living space for them. You'll also be able to interpret whether a social interaction is going well or not. This will go a long way in gaining positive social experiences because you'll be able to intervene before the experience becomes negative with the help of body language interpretation.

The Behaviors that Tell a Story

Body Language

- **Tail wagging** - While wagging is often associated with happiness, it can indicate excitement, anxiety, or aggression. Consider the context and accompanying body language to determine exactly what message your dog is trying to convey.

- **Ears** - Forward-facing ears can indicate attentiveness or excitement, while flattened ears may signal they are scared or are being submissive.

- **Posture** - A relaxed posture with a wagging tail typically signals a content dog. A tense body, raised hackles, or a lowered body may indicate discomfort or aggression.

Vocalization

- **Barking** - Dogs bark for various reasons, including alerting, playfulness, anxiety, or a desire for attention. Take note of the pitch when your dog barks, as well as the intensity and the frequency. They may be sending a message of distress.

- **Whining** - Whining can express excitement, frustration, or anxiety. Context is crucial for clear interpretation.

Social Behavior

- **Pack Instinct** - Dogs are pack animals, and understanding their social structure helps interpret behavior. Depending on the situation, they may exhibit dominance, submission, or cooperation.

- **Play Behavior** - Play is a crucial aspect of dog behavior. Playful actions, such as bowing, signal the dog is in a friendly and non-aggressive mood.

Aggression and Fear

- **Aggressive Behavior** - Aggression can stem from fear, territorial instincts, or discomfort. Signs include growling, baring teeth, and lunging. Identify triggers and address them appropriately.

- **Fearful Behavior** - Fear may manifest as cowering, trembling, or avoidance. Building trust and providing positive experiences can help alleviate fear.

Training and Obedience

- **Response to Commands** - Observe how your dog responds to commands. Consistent training builds communication and reinforces positive behaviors.

- **Reinforcement** - Dogs respond well to positive reinforcement such as treats, praise, or toys. It strengthens desired behaviors.

- Environmental Factors

- **Stressors** - Identify environmental stressors that may affect your dog's behavior, such as loud noises or new experiences.

- **Territorial Behavior** - Dogs may display territorial behavior, such as barking or marking to establish and protect their space.

Health and Well-Being

- **Changes in Behavior** - Sudden changes in behavior could signal health issues. Consult a veterinarian if your dog exhibits sudden, unexpected, or concerning behaviors.

- **Routine and Exercise** - Dogs benefit from routine and regular exercise. Behavioral issues can arise from boredom or lack of physical activity.

Understanding Breed Characteristics

- **Breed Traits** - Different breeds have distinct characteristics and temperaments. Understanding your dog's breed can provide insights into their behavior.

Bonding and Trust

- **Building Trust** - Building a strong bond based on trust and positive interactions fosters a healthier relationship with your dog. Spend quality time together and engage in activities that they enjoy.

Age and Developmental Stages

- **Puppy behavior** - Puppies may exhibit high energy, exploration, and teething behaviors. Consider your pup's age and developmental stage when you begin training them via the clicker training method.

Reading Your Dog's Signals

When you're trying to interpret what signals your dog is giving you, or what their unusual behavior might mean, it is important to consider several things. Firstly, what environment are they in? Are they at home where they're normally calm and comfortable? Are they in a new public environment with many new sounds and smells? A difference in environment, even if only slight, can mean a significant difference in the signal your dog is giving you.

Watch for patterns of behavior. Do they normally get excited when you go for a ride in the car? Do they normally hide when it's time for a bath? Taking note of what is normal behavior for your dog in certain scenarios can help you determine if their behavior is off or not. If they are deviating from normal behavior, it is likely safe to assume their tail's motion (or lack thereof)something isn't right.

Look at your dog's entire body when you're trying to determine how they're feeling at a particular moment. The combination of their ear position, their tail's motion (or lack thereof), and the look in their eyes will tell a story collectively. They might hover over their bowl of frozen food except for the slight wag of their tail and let out a slight growl while your new puppy approaches them. And the message might be, "I'm being patient with you, new puppy, but it won't last long if you get any closer while I'm eating."

Building Trust and Communication

Because building trust and communication with your dog is so important to a long, happy, and healthy relationship, we've put together some exercises. Practicing these often ensures you can use them when you're not clicker training to build up these skills. Practicing these often ensures that your clicker training goes smoothly and only enhances the joy you experience spending time together.

- **Hand Feeding** - This will build a positive association between your hands and food, promoting trust. You can hand feed your dog their meals by offering the food from your palm. Hand feeding will connect specifically with the clicker and treat reward system throughout this training program.

- **Name Recognition** - Use your dog's name by repeatedly calling them gently and positively throughout the day. It will strengthen their bond with you and reinforce their responsiveness in various situations.

- **Eye Contact** - This exercise will also strengthen the bond between dog and owner as well as increase their focus and attention. Hold a treat near your eyes, and when your dog makes eye contact, click a clicker and reward them. Gradually increase the duration of the eye contact before clicking and rewarding them with a treat.

- **Trust Walks** - Trust walks will build up the relationship between you and your dog as well as establish your leadership. Go for a walk with a loose leash. Allow them some freedom while maintaining control. Reward them with a click and a treat when they return to your side to check in with you occasionally.

- **Positive Touch and Massage** - Establish positive associations with your touch and enhance relaxation for your dog. Gently stroke and massage your dog along their head, chest, their belly, back, and legs. When they show signs of enjoyment or relaxation, give them a click and a treat to reward them.

- **Interactive Play** - This bonding exercise is fun for both the dog and the owner. Use a toy that they are familiar with and enjoy to play tug-of-war or fetch. Give them affection and praise when they engage or bring the toy back.

- **Novel Experiences** - These build trust by exposing your dog to new and positive experiences. Gradually introduce your dog to new environments, objects, and people. Be sure to click and reward their trust in you and their curiosity in what's new.

- **Relaxation Exercises** - This will strengthen the bond with your pup deeply and meditatively. After teaching them to lie down, give them positive attention with a soft touch and a soothing voice. Gradually increase the time duration of the relaxation sessions. These can also help with anxiety for your pup.

- **Recall Training** - This will reinforce the communication and bond with your dog by bringing their full attention and focus back to you in various situations. When you have your dog off-leash in a new environment, call their name and use the "come" command. Repeating the recall at various distances and with several different distractions will increase their awareness of you as their leader regardless of the surroundings.

- **Crate Training** - This exercise isn't for everyone, but when done responsibly, it can help bring your pup a sense of safety and trust with you. Create a comfortable space in the crate with soft bedding and toys or treats they enjoy. Encourage them to spend time in it whether you're home or not so that it becomes their safe space when you're out.

Remember that trust and communication are built over time, and each dog is unique. Tailor these exercises to suit your dog's personality and preferences, and enjoy the process of strengthening your bond. Because the bonding process with your dog is ongoing, patience is important. Take every opportunity to celebrate small victories, and remember that the benefits of developing trust and a strong bond with your dog through the clicker training method are not just for them but for you as well. Dogs are unwaveringly loyal and can cure loneliness in a heartbeat. Interacting with your dog can reduce stress and anxiety in the owner, which can alleviate symptoms of depression. Doing these training exercises with your dog will get you moving as well. Physical activity is beneficial to both your physical and mental well-being. Caring for your dog gives a sense of purpose and adds meaning to one's life. They also promote the release of hormones associated with improved mood and can contribute to a more positive outlook on life. Owning and engaging in activities with your dog will also provide opportunities for social interactions. Creating relationships with other dog owners can lead to a feeling of community and wholeness. Besides the benefits already mentioned, your dog will love you unconditionally and do everything in their power to keep you safe. They'll help keep you present in the moment and enjoy the pleasantries of the training experience. They will motivate you when life gets difficult to manage. And they'll provide your life with some routine and structure, which can be comforting to everyone. Building the bonding experience is a symbiotic process where you both come through better than when you started. The companionship of your pup will make for irreplaceable life experiences. Should you encounter challenges while training, consider seeking guidance from a professional dog trainer or veterinarian. Your newly found community of dog lovers can likely help to support you through tougher times as well.

Chapter 8:

Training for Specific Needs

Service or Assistance Dog Training

For service dogs (or assistance dogs, as they're known in some countries), training involves preparing dogs to complete particular tasks and support individuals with disabilities. These highly trained dogs assist people with various disabilities, including hearing loss, diminished eyesight, mental or psychological disabilities, individuals suffering from epilepsy, or who have balance issues. Several conditions benefit from the amazing skills that service dogs learn in their training. Aside from providing care and increased quality of life, service dogs also provide companionship and love. Here are some common types of assistance dogs and the tasks that they are trained to perform:

Guide Dogs

A guide dog is specially trained to assist individuals with visual impairments or blindness in navigating their surroundings. These specific service dogs are also known as "seeing-eye-dogs." They are trained to guide their handlers around obstacles, indicate elevation changes, and help them safely travel from one location to another. Guide dogs are usually medium to large breeds and are selected for their intelligence, temperament, and physical fitness. Some common breeds chosen as guide dogs are Labrador Retrievers, Golden Retrievers, and German Shepherds.

Guide dogs undergo extensive and specialized training to perform specific tasks and ensure the safety of their handlers. The training covers basic obedience in chapter four and advanced mobility and socialization training. The dogs must be able to stay calm and focused while working. Clicker training is extended into the guide dog programs for behaviors such as targeting or locating an empty chair to sit in, indicating where the pedestrian crossing buttons are located, where a curb starts, and several other behaviors that assist the visually impaired owner throughout everyday life. Guide dogs are also trained in "intelligent disobedience." This means that the dog will not follow a command if it means that it will put the handler in danger. Handlers are placed with their guide dog based on the severity of their disability and their lifestyle. Once a guide dog is placed with their handler, ongoing training and support for the pair is continued. The success of the relationship becomes a team effort. Guide dogs significantly enhance the independence and mobility of their handlers and allow them to navigate the world more safely and confidently. The training and partnership between a handler and their guide dog are integral to the success of the assistance relationship.

Hearing Dogs

A hearing dog is a type of service dog specifically trained to assist the deaf and people with hearing impairments. They are trained to alert their handlers to important sounds and signals in the environment, such as doorbells, alarms, phones, the handler's name being called, and other important auditory cues. Hearing dogs are not chosen for their specific breed or size but rather for their temperament, intelligence, and suitability for the individual's lifestyle. Different types of Retrievers and cocker spaniels are a couple of commonly used examples.

Training for hearing dogs includes the basic obedience training found in chapter four but also includes specialized socialization and public access skills. They will use these skills to assist their handlers in being more aware of their surroundings while staying calm, focused, and well-behaved in various public settings. Communication between dogs and handlers is accomplished through a system of cues and alerts. Dogs may use physical signals, such as nudging or pawing, to get their handler's attention. Alert training teaches the dog to provide a specific alert that is associated with a particular sound, which is why the learned physical cues are so important. They are trained even further for scenarios where it would be appropriate to either lead their handler to or away from the sound. In turn, the handlers learn to recognize, interpret, and respond to the specific signals performed by their hearing dogs.

The relationship that is formed between a handler and their hearing dog is built on trust and understanding. Handlers must be confident that their partner will provide vital information about their auditory environment. Hearing dogs enhance the independence and safety of the individuals they're paired with. The training and commitment to the relationship between the handler and the hearing dog are essential to the success of the service partnership.

Seizure Response Dogs

Seizure response dogs are trained and paired with individuals who need assistance with epilepsy or seizure disorders. The purpose of a seizure response dog is not to predict seizures but rather to provide comfort and support to their partner before, during, and after a seizure episode. The dogs are highly trained to respond appropriately when seizures occur, such as fetching assistance devices or seeking help.

These particular service dogs are not chosen for their breed, but similar breeds to other service dogs are common choices, such as retrievers. Standard poodles are also often chosen for the job of seizure response dogs due to their intelligence and temperaments. They are responsible for actions during a seizure that can help keep the handler safe, such as activating an alarm or fetching seizure medication.

Seizure response dogs are trained to recognize signs or behaviors that indicate a seizure is coming on in their handler. Also, the handlers are taught to give their service dogs particular hand signals to tell them that they can feel a seizure is about to start. The communication between a handler and a seizure response dog is critical and may mean life or death for the handler. This is why the training process by which the service dog is trained is also transpired to the handler.

Diabetic Alert Dogs

Diabetic Alert Dogs (DAD) is a support canine that assists individuals with diabetes by detecting changes in blood sugar levels. They are trained to recognize the difference in scents associated with hypoglycemia (low blood sugar) or hyperglycemia (high blood sugar) and can alert their handlers to these changes. The goal is to provide an early warning, allowing individuals with diabetes to take necessary measures, such as administrating insulin or consuming glucose, to manage their blood sugar levels and avoid potential health complications.

DAD companions can detect subtle changes in blood sugar through their handler's breath and body. They are then trained to give a nudge or paw to their handler to indicate that they should take appropriate measures to avoid a diabetic event that can cause confusion, drowsiness, lightheadedness, or loss of consciousness. The handler also learns about the DAD's training so that they can recognize when they are being given an alert and take the necessary preventative actions.

Clicker training for DAD includes a series of scent recognition exercises. Programs that train these dogs professionally will use scent samples and click and reward the dogs for showing initial interest. They then pair the scents with particular alerts from the animal. For example, an extremely low blood sugar scent might be paired with a nose touch to the handler, while a higher blood sugar level might be indicated via a paw touch. The scent and alert pairings are reinforced with a click and a treat. The dogs are introduced to real-life scenarios once the scent recognition and alerts are properly reinforced. The training is reinforced through several repetition exercises in various environments and situations to ensure that the same behaviors are exhibited regardless of the circumstances. Over time, the treats arc phased out of the training process to ensure that the desired behaviors continue even when the handler cannot reward their companion.

Proper communication and training between a DAD and the handling partner creates an opportunity for diabetics to share some of the heavy responsibilities of managing their diabetes with a life companion who is loving and loyal. Thus, it is essential that any service dog trained in the clicker method they are paired with an individual who can continue the training reinforcement and conditioning using the same method. The weight of the relationship, based solely on trust and reliable communication, makes for an enriching and irreplaceable companionship.

Autism Assistance Dogs

Autism Assistance Dogs are also known as Autism Service Dogs. They provide support to individuals with challenges such as sensory sensitivities, social difficulties, and safety concerns. The service dogs trained in Autism support can assist by recognizing when their handler is experiencing a sensory overload and respond by exhibiting calming behaviors. They are also trained to help prevent their handler from wandering or bolting using a tethering system learned during training. Alternatively, they assist with navigating social scenes by offering a comforting and non-judgmental presence.

Like other service dogs, they are not chosen based on breed but on intelligence and temperament. Training includes the same basic obedience training these service dogs complete helps them described in Chapter Four and is enhanced to include socialization, sensory, and task-specific training. The primary goal of training for Autism Assistance Dogs is that they stay calm, focused, and well-behaved in public settings. The sensory training these service dogs complete helps them recognize their dog's cues and respond to specific cues such as pressure stimulation, deep pressure stimulation, or tactile stimulation to recognize sensory sensitivities. The dogs then respond to the cues by providing appropriate support or intervention if necessary.

Continued support and education of both the service dog and their handler is critical to ensure consistent and reliable responsiveness. Individuals greatly benefit from Autism Assistance Dogs through the trust and emotional bond that is built throughout the relationship. The canine partner is tasked with being sensitive and responsive, while the handler recognizes their dog's cues and maintains clear and concise communication. The combination of efforts on both parts results in a valuable and enjoyable relationship.

Psychiatric Service Dogs

Psychiatric service dogs are specialty-trained service animals like many of those mentioned so far. They tend to be chosen for similar reasons, non-breed related but rather intellect and demeanor dependent. Psychiatric service dogs are also trained similarly, including basic obedience, socialization, and task-oriented behaviors.

The difference to note with psychiatric service dogs is that they are trained for a larger variety of indicators. Their primary job is to provide comfort, support, and grounding to their handler regardless of the circumstances. In some situations, the support dog is also tasked with retrieving the appropriate medication in response to emergencies. They can be trained to sense changes in their handler's physiology or behavior and provide an alert before or during a panic attack. The service canine can also be trained to intervene when their handler engages in harmful behaviors such as self-harm or repetitive and destructive actions. They provide physical contact, such as nudging or other grounding techniques, when their handler needs help to calm down, such as when they are experiencing a dissociative episode. Handlers can learn to cue their service dog to retrieve specific medications that they need. The psychiatric service dog can be trained to assist their handlers in public spaces that might otherwise induce anxiety or stress.

The clicker training method is a great training method for psychiatric service dogs and their handlers because it provides the means of consistent and clear communication regardless of the verbal capabilities of the handler. The dogs can learn to respond appropriately and continue to learn even if verbal indicators are impossible. If the individual they are assisting cannot perform the training cues needed, then the caregiver of the individual with psychiatric disabilities is trained as a handler instead. In these cases, the relationship could be shared between the service animal, the caregiver, and the disabled individual. Considering the complexity of the relationship dynamic, the communication, trust, and bond must be securely formed and maintained to ensure a successful experience.

Allergy-Alert Dogs

Individuals who are susceptible to deadly allergies can benefit from enlisting an allergy-alert dog. The dogs are trained to detect the presence of allergens and alert their handlers before they are exposed. The dogs have to be trained to the specific allergen of their handler and be able to indicate its presence regardless of situation, environment, or distractions.

Allergy-alert dogs are trained similarly to diabetic-alert dogs in that scent training is utilized to recognize the particular allergen they are meant to identify. Regarding clicker training, the click and reward system is used when dogs pair recognition with a desired alert cue. The cue can be a nudge or paw of the service dog to their handler. The interpretation of the service dog's alert is equally important to detecting the allergen and alternating the handler. Allergy-alert dogs are trained to signal the presence of an allergen in a variety of settings, environments, and delivery mechanisms. However, miscommunication can lead to a medical emergency if the handler does not properly learn their service animal's signals. In the case of an emergency, they can also be trained to retrieve emergency allergy medication or signal an alarm for help

Allergy-alert dogs can significantly enhance the safety and confidence of individuals with severe allergies by providing additional protection via scent detection training. Their warnings and responsiveness make them invaluable life-long partners. Individuals with severe allergies and their designated allergy-alert dogs can enjoy companionship and a mutually loving relationship with proper training and ongoing conditioning.

Mobility Assistance Dogs

Mobility assistance dogs are also referred to as mobility service dogs. As their title indicates, they are specialty-trained dogs that assist individuals with physical disabilities. Their responsibilities include retrieving items, opening doors, turning on lights, and providing stability. There are no particular breeds that are utilized as mobility assistance dogs, but they are chosen based partially on size and strength due to the taskwork that they are responsible for performing.

Besides the basic obedience training and socialization training, mobility assistance dogs complete extensive task-based training to perform a variety of behaviors that their handler may need assistance with. The clicker-based training method is ideal for mobility assistance dogs because it takes little physical effort to click and reward the desired behaviors. It also provides a sound foundation for clear communication that is necessary for a successful relationship between the service dog and their owner. Task training includes exercises such as retrieving dropped keys or a cell phone, pulling doors open, pressing buttons for automatic doors, turning lights off or on, and supporting an individual should they experience instability while walking or standing. Mobility assistance dogs are also trained to help with transfers for individuals who need to move from seated to standing positions or vice versa. And lastly, in the case of an emergency, mobility assistance dogs can retrieve help or activate an emergency alarm for their handler.

People with physical disabilities who benefit from the partnership of a mobility assistance dog can enjoy more of life's everyday experiences. These service animals promote a more active and autonomous lifestyle. The training and partnership between a handler and a mobility assistance dog are essential for the trust and bond to form in this service relationship.

Medical Alert Dogs

Medical alert dogs are also sometimes referred to as medical detection dogs. These service dogs are trained similarly to diabetic and allergy-alert dogs in that they complete extensive scent training. In addition to the scent training, they are also trained to recognize changes in their handler's body chemistry or behavior that are associated with certain medical conditions.

The training of medical alert dogs consists of the same training as other service dogs, such as basic obedience training, public access training, and socialization in various environments to ensure the dogs will remain focused and well-behaved in various distracting settings. They are then trained with specifications of the medical needs that their handler is susceptible to. These responsibilities may include fetching medical devices or medications, providing emotional support, or indicating to their handler that a medical episode may occur. Some of the medical conditions these service animals can assist with are cardiac conditions and migraines.

Trust within the relationship between a medical alert dog and their owner is critical for assistance training to be beneficial. The handler needs to be in tune with their service animal and be able to understand their cues promptly. In turn, the service dog needs to be able to effectively communicate with their handler when they detect medical-related changes so that the handler can take appropriate action to avoid a medical emergency. The training method adopted must be one that can deliver precise information understood immediately by the dog and handler, such as the clicker training method.

Therapy Dog Training

There is a place for clicker method training throughout all service dog types described so far. Variations of what the service animals learn have been outlined in their summaries. However, the training steps involving clicker training for a therapy dog can be altered and applied to any of the service dogs described in this chapter. Below is an example of how clicker training can be applied to service dog tasks and behaviors.

A therapy dog is trained for preparing them to provide comfort, companionship, and support to individuals in various settings, such as hospitals, nursing homes, schools, and therapy sessions. Therapy dog training is a comprehensive process that involves both the dog and the handler. It is essential to approach the training with dedication and empathy and focus on creating positive and meaningful interactions during the therapy visits. Steps and considerations to train a therapy dog are as follows:

1. **Temperament Assessment** - Ensure the dog has a calm, gentle, and friendly temperament. They should be comfortable in various environments and with different people. Assess their reaction to new situations, loud noises, and crowds.

2. **Basic Obedience Training** - Complete chapter four's Basic Obedience Training exercises to establish a foundation for good behavior and responsiveness to commands. The sit, stay, down, come,

and leave commands are essential. Also, it is important that they have polite leash manners and can walk on a loose leash.

3. **Socialization** - Expose the dog to various people and situations to build their confidence. The experiences should include walking on different surface textures and exposure to different sounds, smells, and settings. They should be able to interact with people of various ages, including children and seniors. When the dog shows calm interest and willingness to acclimate, use the clicker and reward them with treats whenever possible.

4. **Desensitization to Medical Equipment** - Familiarize the dog with medical equipment they may encounter during visits. They should have exposure to wheelchairs, crutches, canes, and hospital beds. Unusual sounds and scents associated with medical practices should also be included in the desensitization process. Use a click and reward for every effort to investigate new surroundings and equipment. Then click and reward for sitting and staying to reinforce calmness.

5. **Comfort with Handling** - Use repeated clicks and rewards during opportunities for new people to gently touch the dog's ears, paws, and tail. Encourage them to be petted by strangers as long as the person is being gentle and respectful of the dog.

6. **Calm Behavior in Various Settings** - If you're able, expose your dog via ride-along or visit emergency care-type settings with loud noises, large crowds, sudden movements, alarms, and emergency equipment. Always carry the clicker and treats so you can encourage calm and collected behaviors in various settings.

7. **Canine Good Citizen (CGC) Certification** - The CGC certification is often a prerequisite for therapy dog programs. They need to be able to demonstrate good manners in public. The CGC certification test includes various obedience and socialization exercises, which should incorporate the considerations outlined thus far in this section.

8. **Therapy Dog-Specific Training** - These particular training programs will teach therapy dogs how to do their work. They will be expected to greet and interact with new people politely, remain calm

during unexpected sounds and disturbances, and follow commands even when distracted.

9. **Volunteer Visits** - Provide supervised visits to practice in real therapy settings. Accompanied the dog during initial visits to ensure comfort and success. Gradually increase their independence as the dog becomes more experienced.

10. **Handlers Training** - Therapy dog handlers should be trained on the proper etiquette and communication during visits. They need to be able to read the dog's body language and understand the needs of the individuals that are being visited.

11. **Health Check-ups** - Ensure the dog is in good health and up-to-date on vaccinations. Regular veterinary visits can help adhere to vaccination and health requirement standards the therapy dog program sets.

12. **Insurance and Liability** - Appropriate insurance should be taken out to cover liability protection. Some therapy dog programs or facilities may require insurance, but you'll want to confirm with the program and facility's (where you'll be doing the visits) legal and insurance policies.

13. **Certification** - Therapy dog programs will require official certification from a recognized organization, such as Therapy Dogs International (TDI), Pet Partners, and the CGC mentioned previously.

14. **Continued Training** - Therapy dogs should have ongoing training and exposure to new experiences. They should participate in regular training sessions and attend workshops or seminars that build on the therapy dog skills that they have already developed.

Chapter 9:

Maintaining and Generalizing

Behaviors

The Importance of Consistency

Dogs thrive on consistency because it provides clear communication. When commands, cues, and expectations are consistent, dogs can better understand what is expected of them. Inconsistent signals or responses can confuse them and hinder the learning process. Consistency helps in establishing a routine for dogs. They are creatures of habit and feel more secure and confident when they know what to expect, much like their human companions. Consistent feeding times, walking schedules, and training routines contribute to a stable environment.

Positive reinforcement relies on consistency. If a behavior is rewarded every time it occurs, the dog associates that behavior with a positive outcome. Inconsistent reinforcement can lead to confusion and uncertainty about which behaviors are desirable.

Consistency builds trust between the dog and the handler. Dogs feel more secure than their environment, and interactions are consistent. This trust is essential for a strong dog and owner bond. Dogs also learn more effectively and more quickly in a consistent training environment. They can make the association faster when they receive the same outcome for a specific behavior each time. Inconsistency can lead to delayed learning or even the learning of undesirable behaviors.

Dogs interpret the world through patterns and associations. Inconsistent commands or responses can confuse them, making it harder for them to understand what is expected. Clarity in communication reduces confusion and promotes faster learning. Consistency is especially crucial when addressing behavioral issues. Whether reinforcing positive behavior or discouraging undesirable behavior, consistent responses are essential for effective behavior modification. Setting and enforcing boundaries consistently is also vital for a well-behaved dog. If a dog is allowed on the couch one day and scolded for it the next, it creates confusion. Clear and consistent rules help the dog understand what is acceptable behavior. Once a behavior is trained, consistency is necessary to maintain it. If a dog is inconsistently reinforced for a learned behavior, the behavior may become unreliable or diminish over time.

Consistency contributes to a positive relationship between the dog and the owner. Predictable interactions create a sense of security for the dog and foster a trusting and respectful relationship. Remember that dogs respond best to routine, clear expectations, and positive reinforcement. Consistency in training and daily interactions creates an environment where dogs can thrive, learn, and develop into well-behaved companions.

Proofing Behaviors in Different Environments

In dog training, "proofing" a behavior refers to the process of strengthening and solidifying a trained behavior under various conditions, distractions, and environments. The goal is to ensure the dog reliably performs the desired behavior in different situations, even when faced with challenges or distractions. Proofing helps generalize the behavior, making it more robust and applicable in real-world scenarios.

Dogs may initially learn a behavior in a specific context or environment. Proofing then takes the same behavior and introduces distractions to the training environment. Distractions could include other dogs, people, noises, or novel objects. The goal is to teach the dog to remain focused on the desired behavior despite external stimuli.

Proofing a behavior may start with going to a different room, going outside, or placing toys in the vicinity while training. We have introduced proofing techniques throughout the basic obedience and advanced training chapters. However, you can take it several steps further in practice. Complex proofing can involve variable timing of the commands and rewards, changing the duration or distance of the behavior you're asking for, changing the conditions under which they must perform the behavior, introducing real-life scenarios, and increasing the difficulty of the behavior you're asking for.

Variable Timing

By varying the timing, dogs learn not to become reliant on a predictable pattern. Introducing variability helps ensure the dog responds consistently, regardless of when the command is given or the reward is provided. For example, follow the steps provided to introduce variable timing into your clicker training program:

1. Initially, when the dog successfully sits on cue, click the clicker immediately and provide a treat. This immediate reinforcement helps the dog quickly associate the click with the desired behavior, such as sitting.

2. After a few repetitions with immediate reinforcement, you can introduce variability by delaying the treat after the click. For example, the dog sits, you click the clicker, and then you wait for a variable amount of time (a difference of seconds) before delivering the treat.

3. In the next repetition, you might click and reward with a treat in quick succession. Reverting to rewarding more quickly after the click will reinforce the desired behavior.

4. Occasionally, you might use a double-click. In this case, the dog sits, you click twice in quick succession, and then provide the treat. The double-click becomes a variation that adds an element of surprise and interest for the dog.

5. Vary the duration between the click and treat. Sometimes it's immediate, and other times there's a slight delay. This variability helps the dog become more resilient to changes in the timing.

6. Implement random reinforcement, where not every correct behavior is followed by a click and a treat. The unpredictability keeps the dog actively offering the behavior in the hope of receiving reinforcement.

7. Occasionally, provide a jackpot reward by offering multiple treats or a particularly high-value treat after a single click. This adds excitement and reinforces the behavior strongly.

8. Example Session:

   A. Dog sits (Click + Treat)

   B. Dog sits (Click + Treat)

   C. Dog sits(Click + Delay + Treat)

   D. Dog sits (Double-Click + Treat)

   E. Dog sits (Click + No Treat)

   F. Dog sits (Click + Quick Succession Treat)

   G. Dog sits (Click + Variable Duration + Treat)

   H. Dog sits (Click + Jackpot Reward)

By incorporating variable timing in clicker training, you make the learning process more engaging and prevent the dog from becoming overly dependent on a fixed pattern. This variability helps the dog generalize the behavior and respond reliably in different situations.

Variable Durations and Distances of the Behavior

When proofing behaviors in training, it is important to introduce many variations, including the duration of the behavior and the distance from which it is done from the handler. In this example, we'll use the clicker training command "stay" and incorporate variable durations and distances.

1. Begin with the dog in a "sit" or a "down" position. Click and treat for a short duration stay, such as one or two seconds. The dog learns that staying in a position is rewarding.

2. Gradually vary the duration of the stay. Click and treat for a three-second stay, then a five-second stay, and so on. Introduce unpredictability in the length of time the dog is expected to stay.

3. Occasionally, quickly click and reward with a treat after issuing the "stay" command. This reinforces the behavior of remaining in place for a short duration.

4. Once the dog is comfortable staying in place for different durations, start to vary the distance between you and the dog. Click and reward with a treat for the short stay, then take a step back before rewarding. Return to the dog to provide the treat.

5. Gradually increase the distance. Click and treat for a stay, take a few steps away, and then return to deliver the treat. This helps the dog learn that staying in a position is rewarding regardless of your proximity.

6. Introduce distractions while varying duration and distance. Click and reward with a treat for staying in place amid distractions, ensuring that the dog maintains focus on the "stay" command.

7. Randomize the duration and distance. Sometimes, click for a short stay with increased distance, and other times for a longer stay with you closer. This keeps the dog engaged and attentive.

8. Introduce a release cue (we have started with this in some of the previous chapters) to indicate to your dog that it is okay to come out of the "stay" command, such as "okay" or "free". Click and treat for a successful stay, then use the release cue to signal the end of the stay.

9. Example Session:

    A. Dog stays for 2 seconds (Click + Treat)

    B. Dog stays for 5 seconds (Click + Treat)

    C. Quick Reinforcement - Dog stays for 3 seconds (Click + Treat)

    D. Dog stays with you a step away (Click + Treat)

    E. Dog stays for 7 seconds with increased distance (Click + Treat)

    F. Quick Reinforcement - Dog stays for 4 seconds (Click + Treat)

    G. Dog stays amid distractions for 6 seconds (Click + Treat)

    H. Release cue - "Okay" (Click + Treat)

You teach the dog to perform the same behavior under different conditions by incorporating variable durations and distances. This helps build a reliable and adaptable behavior in various situations.

Changing Conditions

Changing conditions in clicker training involves introducing variations and challenges to the training environment, helping the dog associate the ask with the desired behavior more reliably in different situations. Here's an example using the "sit" command to illustrate changing conditions in clicker training:

1. Start the training indoors in a quiet environment. Issue the "sit" command, click, and reward with a treat when the dog complies. Repeat until the dog reliably sits indoors.

2. Move the training session outdoors. The change in environment introduced new smells, sounds, and distractions. Practice the "sit" command, click, and reward with a treat.

3. Change the surface the dog is sitting on. Move from a flat floor to a carpeted area or a grassy patch. This helps the dog generalize the behavior to various textures.

4. Have different people issue the "sit" command. This helps the dog learn to respond to cues from various family members or friends. Click and reward with a treat for successful sits.

5. Train in different weather conditions. If it's raining or windy, practice the "sit" command outdoors. This will help the dog maintain consistency with the responding behavior regardless of the conditions.

6. Conduct training sessions during different times of the day to adjust them to the different lighting of day and night. Click and reward with treats if they comply with the "sit" behavior in the early morning, twilight, and nighttime hours.

7. Vary your posture when giving the "sit" command. Try standing on a table or chair, sitting on the floor, or slumping in bed. The

dog will learn that the same behavior is expected regardless of what position you're in.

8. Lastly, several changing conditions are combined to provide a more solid expectation of the desired behavior. You can practice the sit command from bed in a dark room, have a friend or family member use the "sit" command when it is raining outside, and so on. Use your imagination to come up with a variety of combinations for your dog to try.

9. Example Session:

   A. Indoor sit (Click + Treat)

   B. Outdoor sit on the grass (Click + Treat)

   C. Sit on another textured surface (Click + Treat)

   D. Family member gives the sit command (Click + Treat)

   E. Sit during light rain (Click + Treat)

   F. Sit at night with a different posture (Click + Treat)

   G. A friend gives the sit command at the park (Click + Treat)

By incorporating changing conditions in clicker training, you help the dog realize that the behavior being asked of them is the same regardless of their surroundings or situation. This approach prepares the dog for real-world scenarios where conditions may not always be consistent, promoting a well-rounded and adaptable response to commands.

Real-World Scenarios

Teaching real-world scenarios in dog training is essential for several reasons, as it helps dogs become well-rounded and adaptable in various situations. Dogs initially learn behaviors in specific training environments. They then begin experiencing some alternative environments when the trainer asks for the same behavior outside versus inside, with distractions in the room such as toys, or when they have a friend or family member ask for the same learned behavior. These are all important exercises leading up to real-world scenarios where the behaviors will be put to the ultimate test. Dogs that are trained only in controlled environments may struggle to adapt to real-world situations. Training in various scenes helps dogs become more adaptable, confident, and capable of behaving appropriately regardless of where they are or what is going on around them.

An example of a real-world scenario introduction to clicker training may go as follows:

1. We'll use the "recall" or "come" command for this example. The training starts indoors with minimal distractions. The "come" command is reliably reinforced with a click and a treat.

2. The training session is moved outdoors, maybe to the backyard, and greater distances are incorporated in the "come" command. Clicks and rewards are consistent until the command and behavior are reliable.

3. Next, the "come" command is practiced in a public setting, such as at a park. The change in environment introduces new smells, sounds, and potential distractions. Initial recalls in this new environment can be practiced on a long leash. As the behavior becomes more reliable, the leash can be removed, increasing the distance gradually.

4. Practice the "come" command when new people are giving your pup attention. This helps them learn that they are still expected to comply with the command even if they are receiving affection and/or praise from others.

5. Practice the "come" command in a variety of weather patterns and practice it randomly amongst play activities. This teaches the dog that the "come" command can happen anytime and

anywhere, and the behavior is expected to be the same. Click
and reward all successful recalls.

6. Lastly, practice the "come" command from unexpected
   locations. Go to a friend's house or an office building and
   remove yourself from sight. Click and reward with a treat when
   your dog comes to find you.

7. Example Session:

   A. Recall indoors (Click + Reward)

   B. Recall outdoors (Click + Reward)

   C. Recall at the park (Click + Reward)

   D. Recall around new people (Click + Reward)

   E. Recall near other dogs (Click + Reward)

   F. Recall in different weather (Click + Reward)

   G. Recall from play (Click + Reward)

   H. Recall from out of sight (Click + Reward)

By incorporating real-world scenarios into clicker training, you take away
the uncertainty of what is expected from them when conditions change.
This approach ensures that the dog responds reliably to the command
every time and enhances their safety as well as your ability to manage
them effectively in different settings.

Keeping Up with Training as Your Dog Ages

A dog's age can significantly impact their training in various ways. A dog's developmental stage and life experiences influence how they learn and respond to training.

Puppyhood (Up to 6 Months)

- **Critical Learning Period** - Puppyhood is a critical time for learning and socialization. Puppies are sponges for information and can quickly pick up on basic commands and social cues.

- **Short Attention Span** - Puppies have shorter attention spans than grown dogs, so training sessions should be brief and engaging (maximum of 5 minutes). The focus of the training sessions should always be positive reinforcement.

- **Socialization Priority** - Socialization is crucial during this period. Exposure to various people, environments, and other animals helps prevent fear and aggression issues later in life.

- **Basic Commands** - Start with the basic obedience commands outlined in chapter four. Consistency and positive reinforcement are key.

- **Introduction to Leash and Crate Training** - Introduce walking on a leash and crate training early to encourage normalcy and establish good habits.

Adolescence (6 Months to 2 Years)

- **Testing Boundaries** - Adolescents may test boundaries and exhibit behaviors like chewing or digging. Consistent training, exercise, and redirection should help to manage these tendencies.

- **Energy Levels** - Adolescents often have high levels of energy. Regular exercise is essential for channeling their energy in positive ways.

- **Advanced Commands** - Build on basic commands and introduce more advanced ones. Training sessions can be slightly longer as attention spans improve. Gradually work up to training in 10-minute durations.

- **Impulse Control** - Exercises that incorporate extended duration and the introduction of minor distractions can assist with tapering impulse control in adolescent dogs.

- **Socialization** - Introducing your dog to new people, new environments, and even to other well-behaved dogs can increase confidence and reduce anxiety and fear. Dogs respond negatively to fear and anxiety, so helping them become more confident around others will ensure they mind their manners in social situations.

Adulthood (2 Years and Older)

- **Establishing Habits** - Dogs may have established habits by adulthood. Training can still be effective, but breaking ingrained behaviors may take longer. Consistency in their training is crucial to break bad habits and form new ones.

- **Matured Attention Span** - Their attention span has matured by the age of 2 and allows for more complex training sessions. You can introduce more distractions and variations in the training exercises as long as the base of the exercises has been well established beforehand. Mature dogs can excel in advanced training, sports, or activities. Mental stimulation remains important for their well-being.

Senior Years (7 Years and Older)

- **Physical considerations** - Physical limitations may arise, affecting mobility and energy levels. Adjust training as necessary to accommodate the dog's comfort.

- **Cognitive Challenges** - Older dogs may experience cognitive decline. Maintain mental stimulation through gentle training and interactive toys. Sticking to a particular routine can also assist with anxieties formed during cognitive decline, as they will appreciate the predictability.

- Positive Interaction - Older dogs appreciate the emotional connections with their owners. Continue to give them positive reinforcements, affection, and rewards for their efforts even if they don't perform to the extent they used to.

Being patient with your dog through all of life's stages is important. There will be times when your dog will regress or face new challenges. These are the times when consistency and positive reinforcement are most important. You may need to adapt your training approach to suit the needs of your dog, whether they be physical, mental, or age-related. While your dog's age influences their learning abilities, energy levels, and behavioral tendencies, they remain a loyal and loving partner throughout the process and deserve our unwavering commitment in return. Tailor your training methods to accommodate your dog's age, and you're sure to align better with expectations and performance during training sessions.

Chapter 10:

Clicker Training Success Stories

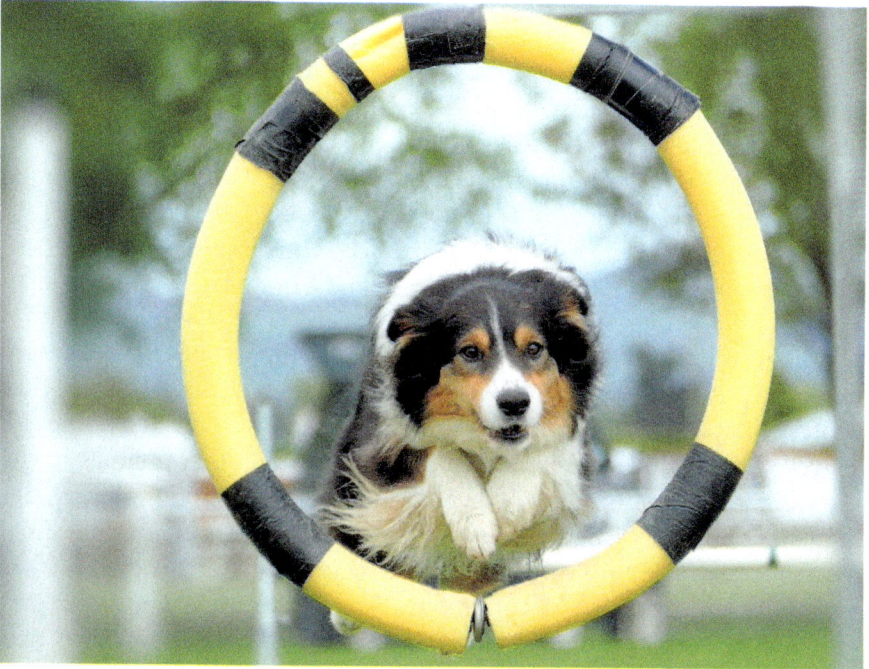

Real-Life Examples of Dogs Successfully Trained with Clicker Methods

La Miette

A beloved dog named La Miette lived in a charming neighborhood nestled between rolling hills and bustling streets debuted. Her story wasn't exactly a fairy tale; it was a real-life testament to the incredible transformations that clicker training could bring to a dog's life.

La Miette, a spirited papillon, started her journey out of a puppy mill, rescued by an unknowing and unsuspecting woman named Virginia. Due to La Miette's minute size, there was soon trouble in the house as she was only the size of a teacup and constantly had to avoid being stepped on by monstrous feet. She soon became skittish and timid of people while also avoiding any human interaction due to her increasing fear and anxiety.

Luckily, Virginia had just attended her first clicker training class only a week before bringing La Miette into her home and quickly saw an opportunity to put her newfound skill to the test. La Miette responded so quickly to the training that she soon mastered advanced exercises. At four months old, she began starring in videos and debuted in Take a Bow Wow, as well as several TV commercials and print ads.

La Miette's rise to stardom was credited to her impeccably rapid learning trajectory, thanks to the clicker training she received. Beyond her professional life, clicker training helped tremendously in her home life as well. She became more well-mannered with the other animals in the house, more comfortable and welcoming of interactions with her humans, and she carried the joy of her training through to her final moments. La Miette was diagnosed with cancer later in life, but her happiness and lust for life continued through the tricks and behaviors she knew so well from her clicker training. Virginia was convinced that clicker training gave her precious pup a sense of purpose and joy. For that reason, she has shared her story of La Miette with the world to inspire others to adopt clicker training as their dog's training method and experience the same rewarding relationship as she did.

Jack

There once was a Border Collie named Jack. Jack's story isn't a conventional one - he faced behavioral challenges that made him difficult to handle. However, through the power of patience, positive reinforcement, and clicker training, Jack's story transforms into one of redemption and hope.

Jack's journey with his owner, Renee, began when she was contacted by a friend to see if she was willing to adopt her 14-month-old Border Collie. Renee lived on a farm and was her friend's only option other than taking him back to the shelter she had originally found him in about a year prior. Renee had visited her friend several times and remembered Jack being routinely tied up or in his crate so as not to "bother" anyone visiting. She also remembered an incident where her friend's 11-year-old son had smacked the dog because he wasn't performing his commands.

Renee went to her friend's house to assess Jack and how he might respond to a kinder handler. She noted that he was fairly easygoing until she went to reach for one of his toys to toss to him. Jack responded with a snap at her, and she realized that he was object-guarding. Considering that this form of aggressive behavior can be dangerous if not properly corrected, Renee had to consult with her husband to decide whether Jack would be welcome in their home or not.

A few weeks later, Renee called her friend to bring Jack to the farm. From that moment on, Jack had a new and permanent home. However, Renee and her husband's journey with Jack wasn't easy. They began with general obedience classes, lots of exercise, and some agility training. The extensive physical activity did help Jack relax a bit, but his object guarding was still a problem.

At one point, Jack bit someone's hand, which caused several puncture wounds. Jack was nearly euthanized when one of the trainers offered to start working with him on a one-on-one basis. That is when Jack and Renee were introduced to the clicker training method. Renee was instructed to click and reward Jack with treats several times daily to help condition the clicker. She kept the rewards highly motivating by using bits of leftovers from the fridge, pieces of hot dogs, and bits of liver.

Renee tag-teamed Jack's training while initially using a basket muzzle to keep him from biting. The trainer would issue the command and the click while Renee gave the treat through the muzzle. It was a bit tricky due to the crucial timing of the click and reward, but they were able to establish a rhythm and work with Jack successfully several times a week.

They eventually came up with a list of Jack's triggers to bite, which included grabbing him by the collar, leaning over him, brushing him anywhere on his body, clipping his toenails, reaching over his head, cleaning or medicating his ears, taking anything away from him, petting him after he was already asleep, making eye contact, looking at him when he had a bone, being at the vet's office, getting injections, reaching in toward him while he was in his crate, and touching his genital area. (Premaza, 2008)

The trainer who worked with Jack and Renee began their clicker training with the use of a prop known as an Assess-a-Hand. It was a training tool with an imitation hand on the end of a long handle. This allowed the trainer to begin desensitizing Jack to touch without the danger of being bitten. Each time Jack would allow the hand to touch him without reacting with a snap, Renee would reward him with a click and a treat. They focused the lessons on positivity and always tried to end with success, even if it was only a small one. Whenever the training seemed to go a little too fast or too far for Jack, and he responded with a snap or a growl, he would not be rewarded. Instead, they would take the exercise back a step to where Jack was comfortable and end the lesson with a click and a treat so he would feel confident and positive about the experience.

Each lesson would start with the positive exercise they had ended in the previous session. Then, they would move on to more challenging exercises. Eventually, the trainer put the Assess-a-Hand away and could start working with Jack without the risk of being bitten. They had formed trust between them that Jack had never experienced with anyone. Renee would testify that she could see Jack putting more and more effort into each lesson and truly enjoying being such a good boy. His behaviors began changing in other ways as well. He began licking them affectionately and making eye contact with a soft expression.

There were several more ups and downs with Jack, but he continuously made progress as Renee continued with his clicker training and desensitizing exercises. Of course, the science isn't perfect, but the clicker training method saved Jack's life. Had he stayed the course with his aggressive tendencies, he would have been euthanized. Luckily, with the help of the clicker, a professional trainer, and a lovingly persistent owner, Jack could adapt most of his behaviors to being safe and socially acceptable. Renee continues to revert to the clicker any time Jack shows signs of being uncomfortable or when she is unsure as to how he might react to a new situation. The clicker has given both Jack and Renee a way of communicating with each other safely and consistently.

Sasha

Sasha's story starts in a small cardboard box brought into a local animal shelter by a man perturbed as to why this little creature would not leave his yard. She was a ray of sunshine who brought out a smile in everyone who crossed her path, as she had a sweet-natured temperament and seemed to smile herself most of the time. However, it was soon discovered that the reason Sasha could not leave the yard of the citizen who brought her in was because her back legs were incapacitated. Were it not for Sasha's sweet personality, it is likely that the adoption center would have decided to put her down.

Though the doctors and staff at the adoption center chose to save Sasha's life, her journey to truly live was still a long one. She was featured on local television hoping someone would adopt her and the community would help financially support the medical attention Sasha needed. As it turned out, Sasha was adopted, but the community support fell through, and eventually, so did her new home. Before long, Sasha was back at the adoption center.

That's when she was found and taken home by a woman named Christina. She was informed of the extensive care Sasha would need but was so motivated by the pup's sweetness that she and her husband embraced the challenge of taking Sasha into their home. With an incredibly supportive husband, who happened to be the son of an engineer, Christina and her husband began making arrangements to have a custom wheelchair built for Sasha.

When the wheelchair arrived, that is when the clicker training began. Christina took her time with Sasha, and though it took several days just to get her comfortably approaching the contraption, eventually, Sasha was voluntarily getting strapped into her wheelchair via clicks and treats. Due to the lack of strength in her front legs, she could not hold herself in a standing position for very long. So, clicker training sessions were kept very short and focused on standing and taking a few steps.

Over time, Sasha was able to build enough strength to support herself in the wheelchair for 15-minute walks. Then, Christina decided to take her for her first walk in the park. Little did she know that the duck pond would be the highly motivating factor to take Sasha from a lazy stroll to a full-out sprint. Now, Christina regularly uses the duck pond to encourage exercise with Sasha. Between the clicker, treats, and duck pond, Sasha has developed enough to run, play, and be equals with her canine friends.

Chapter 11:

Troubleshooting and Common

Pitfalls

Addressing Challenges in Training

Challenges are integral to the training journey when molding a well-behaved and responsive canine. Whether you're working with a puppy, a senior dog, a dog with disabilities, or a rescue pup, challenges are likely to arise. Each dog has a unique history and personality, which will surface several quirks that may or may not be conducive to the training goals.

Lack of Motivation

Dealing with a lack of motivation in dogs during training can be challenging, but with the right approach, you can reignite their interest and enthusiasm. Evaluate the rewards that are offered to your dog and experiment with different types. Discover what truly excites them and then repeat the evaluation whenever you sense the motivation declining again. It might be that the treats used for training are not enticing enough. Or, if they are receiving high-value treats outside of training (possibly table scraps), it might be a good idea to save them for training sessions only.

If you feel as though the treats are not the problem, evaluate aspects of the training sessions, such as their duration and tone. If 10 minutes seems to be too long for your pup, shorten the session to keep their attention. Also, ensure that the training sessions are kept positive and always end on a good note. If you've hit a wall with a particular exercise, take it back a step or two and end the session with a click and reward for something your pup has already mastered. Alternatively, if you've worked on the same exercises for an extended period, it may interest your pet to move on to something new and exciting. Break the new exercise down into bite-sized pieces and give ample opportunity to click and reward even the smallest successes.

After evaluating the treats and the training sessions, if your pup still seems to lack motivation, it may be an indicator of health concerns. Seek professional guidance from a veterinarian to ensure your pup isn't in pain or facing a health-related complication. Alternatively, take them to a professional trainer to see if there are additional tricks of the trade that you can incorporate into your clicker training sessions at home.

Distractions

At some point during the clicker training journey, your dog will likely get distracted. Through the exercises outlined in this book, we've tried to set the stage for distraction-free training. It is important to eventually work through the exercises to the point of introducing distractions and training to them. However, this should be done gradually, as introducing distractions in training too soon can backfire and end up side-tracking their progress.

If you find that your dog is getting distracted regularly, it might be a good time to teach them a "leave it" or "watch me" command. You can also use a long leash if wandering off during the training session seems to be an issue. Introduce a growing distance between yourself and your dog during training so that they become accustomed to following commands regardless of your proximity.

Fear, Anxiety, Reactivity, or Aggression

When a dog struggles with fear or anxiety, it's important to take extra precautions. Ensure the environment is as calming as possible, and encourage your dog to remain calm as well through positive reinforcements. If there is something that triggers fear or anxiety for your pup, very slowly desensitize them through a positive association of clicks and rewards for even the smallest progression. Counterconditioning can be used to relieve some of their fear and anxiety by pairing positive experiences with the trigger for their discomfort. It will help them change their emotional response to the stimuli.

Keep the training sessions short (shorter than the recommended 10 minutes for dogs with fear and anxiety) and always remain calm and patient. Keep movements slow, use a gentle voice, and avoid direct eye contact until they are more comfortable with the experience. Be sure you evaluate what their triggers are and be sensitive to them. Use consistent signals and methods so that they are not surprised during training.

If necessary, consult a veterinarian to discuss calming supplements or aids such as a pheromone diffuser or calming collar to help reduce their anxiety. If they allow you to, try calming touch or massage before and after the training sessions to promote relaxation. Avoid punishments and instead focus on rewarding desired behaviors at every opportunity. And allow them time and space to become comfortable with any training tools before bringing the tool into use.

When training a dog with any degree of fear, anxiety, reactivity, or aggression, it is important to be patient and build their trust gradually. Read their body language to tell you if they feel uncomfortable before reacting and adjust the training accordingly. Progress will likely be slow, but every success is worth celebrating. If you prioritize your dog's well-being throughout the process, they will also respond with trust and respect. If these conditions persist throughout training or become dangerous, seek professional help for additional guidance.

Inconsistency

Inconsistency in dog training can have several negative impacts on a dog's behavior, learning, and the overall effectiveness of the training efforts. Dogs thrive on routine and predictability. Inconsistent commands or responses before the exercise is properly conditioned can confuse them about what is expected. Inconsistency in signals can make it challenging for the dog to understand the desired behavior. Dogs learn through repetition and consistent reinforcement. Inconsistent training can slow down the learning process, as dogs may misunderstand which behavior is being rewarded.

Persistent inconsistencies in training can contribute to the development of behavioral issues. If a dog receives mixed messages, they may exhibit undesirable behaviors in an attempt to interpret what is being asked of them. If the dog is given different responses to the same cue, it can also break down trust in them. Trust and confidence in dogs are built upon the predictability of their owner's actions. When they aren't sure what the response will be for a behavior, they are less motivated to display it. Not only does the trust get damaged by inconsistencies, but it can also induce anxiety and stress in the dog.

Consistency is a cornerstone of successful dog training. It provides a framework for dogs to understand expectations and fosters a positive learning environment. Establishing clear and consistent communication helps dogs feel secure and confident in their interactions with their owners.

Impatience

Impatience can cause quite a bit of damage when training a dog. It can lead to incomplete training sessions, as trainers may cut sessions short or skip steps in an attempt to see quicker results. It can lead to inconsistent commands and cues, which confuses and hinders the dog's learning.

Sometimes, impatience comes from having unrealistic expectations about the speed of progress. Dogs, especially puppies, need time to learn and internalize commands. If you go too quickly for them, you can miss opportunities for them to solidify their learning and potentially encounter a setback. Practice mindfulness during the training sessions to ensure your pup connects the dots along the way. Stay present and focused on the task at hand rather than fixated on desired outcomes.

Boredom

To avoid boredom for you or your canine, be sure to keep to the 10-minute maximum duration for training sessions. If necessary, shorten the sessions to seven or even five minutes and gradually build up to ten minutes as the pup's attention span matures. When you go into the sessions, have a plan by recapping what they learned from the last session and then building a bit of complexity onto it. This way, you'll reinforce learned behaviors while changing the routine to help them grow in their training.

Be sure to keep the sessions fun and engaging. You can do this by switching up the high-value treats they receive as rewards, incorporating play into the sessions by tossing a ball a few times between exercises, and changing the training location when they're ready. If possible, bring family members or friends into the training sessions as well. Not only does this help make training more interesting for your pup and teaches them that the desired behaviors are consistent regardless of who is asking for them.

Medical Issues

Training a dog with medical issues presents unique challenges that require careful consideration. If a dog is experiencing pain or discomfort, then they may be less motivated to engage in training. Watch and take note of certain movements that seem to cause your dog discomfort, as continuing them could exacerbate their condition. If they are experiencing chronic pain from conditions such as arthritis, their physical abilities may be limited. Help protect them from further damage by avoiding exercises they have a hard time doing.

As dogs age, they may experience reduced stamina or cognitive impairments that affect their training sessions. While we wouldn't recommend sessions last any longer than 10 minutes, it may be appropriate to shorten them further. Cognitive impairments may limit their attention span or understanding of more complex exercises. Keeping training sessions short and simple should help them stay engaged and moderately active.

While training provides an avenue for physical and mental growth for your pup, monitor their abilities closely and tailor the training sessions accordingly. Set realistic goals and expectations for the training sessions and be very patient if it takes longer than anticipated for them to perform the desired behavior. Take short breaks between exercises if they seem to tire easily, and remember that there is no one-size-fits-all approach to training. They will rely on you to determine when they have done well, so to keep the sessions positive and productive, reward them with a click and a treat at every opportunity.

Mistakes to Avoid

- **Inconsistent Timing** - Clicking too early or too late can confuse your dog and make it challenging for them to understand which behavior is being rewarded. Practice precise timing to ensure the click coincides with the exact moment your dog performs the desired behavior. Also, if family members or friends are included in the training, either do the clicking for them or ensure they are well informed about the importance of the timing when clicking the clicker.

- **Overusing the Clicker** - Be sure not to click the clicker too often without rewarding it with a treat as well. It can diminish the click's value and result in confusion and a loss of motivation from your pup. Use the clicker selectively, pair it with rewards consistently, and reserve the click for marking the desired behavior.

- **Inadequate Reinforcement** - Providing insufficient or inconsistent reinforcement can lead to your dog's lack of motivation and interest. Use high-value treats and ensure that the reinforcement is meaningful. Gradually reduce the frequency of the treats as the behavior becomes more established.

- **Skipping Basic Training Steps** - Skipping foundational steps in training and moving too quickly to advanced behaviors can result in confusion and frustration for your pup. Establish a solid foundation by reinforcing basic commands and moving through them slowly before progressing to the more advanced exercises.

- **Not Staying Positiv**e - Though clicker training with your dog will have its ups and downs, staying lighthearted and positive throughout the process is important. If you're not having fun, then it's likely that your dog isn't either. If there is a lack of consistency, too many distractions during the sessions, or a failure to recognize adjustments that need to be made to suit the specific needs of your dog, then it can result in the training sessions feeling stressful, which is counterproductive to the desired training outcomes. Keep the sessions short and fun, and reward your dog often. Keep an eye out for when they might need a break, a bit more clicker conditioning, or a refresher on the basics. Always end the sessions on a positive note.

Frustrations and Setbacks

Frustration and setbacks are a normal part of the learning process for the dogs and their owners in clicker training. Understanding the challenges and mistakes to avoid will help limit some of these occurrences, but a few are bound to pop up. Be patient and realistic about what you set out to achieve with your particular dog. Try to avoid comparing them with what other dogs can achieve and instead focus on their specific abilities. If you notice that your dog's behaviors are inconsistent or that they are reverting to previous behaviors, then it may be time to go back to the basics and do more reinforcement. Things may be moving a bit too quickly for them. It is easy to overwhelm them with too much information if things become too complex in a shorter period. Stay calm and positive. If frustration sets in, take a break and regroup. Training should be enjoyable for both you and your dog. Maintain a positive mindset and focus on the progress they've made.

Conclusion and Ongoing Training

The journey of clicker training is a symphony of small victories, a dance between two beings eager to understand each other. As you embark on this path, it's essential to celebrate not only the destination but each step, recognizing that the journey is, in fact, a lifelong adventure.

Clicker training is a conversation, a language shared between you and your canine companion. With each click and treat, a connection is forged, and the harmony of success echoes through the training sessions. As your dog grasps new commands and refines behaviors, the sense of accomplishment is palpable, a shared joy that strengthens your bond.

In the world of clicker training, no victory is too small. Whether it's a perfectly executed sit or a recall amidst distractions, take a moment to revel in these achievements. The click becomes a musical note, punctuating the melody of progress. Consider the click as applause, a standing ovation for your dog's efforts. The click marks the exact moment of success, acknowledging their understanding and executing the desired behavior. Success breeds confidence, and confidence is the cornerstone of a well-trained dog. Each successful click builds your dog's assurance in their ability to understand and respond, paving the way for more advanced training.

Recognize that training is not a finite endeavor but a lifelong journey. Dogs, like humans, continue to learn and adapt throughout their lives. The clicker becomes a lifelong companion, a tool for communication that evolves with each stage of your dog's development. Life is dynamic, and so is the training journey. Changes in routine, environment, or the introduction of new family members require adaptation. Clicker training becomes a flexible language, adjusting to the ever-shifting rhythms of life.

Lifelong training involves advanced commands and complex behaviors. As your dog matures, you can introduce more intricate training exercises, keeping their mind sharp and engaged. Dogs undergo behavioral changes throughout their lives, much the same as we do. Lifelong clicker training gives you the platform to address those changes and reinforce positive behaviors while modifying undesirable ones. This deepens the connection between you and your dog. The more you communicate through the clicker, the richer and more nuanced your relationship becomes.

Acknowledging that setbacks are part of the journey is crucial for a resilient training approach. The clicker becomes the guiding light that steers you through rough waters when challenges arise, whether due to environmental factors, health issues, or behavioral changes. Setbacks are opportunities for reassessment and modification. If a particular behavior proves challenging, the clicker training method allows you to break it down into smaller, more manageable steps.

Remember to practice patience and persistence. Dogs may not grasp a concept immediately. Consistent training, marked with a click, reinforces the importance of patience. For example, teaching your dog to walk politely on a leash requires persistence. The click becomes the motivational beat, encouraging you and your dog to continue working toward success.

As your journey with the clicker unfolds, there comes a point when the legacy of learning extends beyond your current dog. The knowledge, skills, and communication established through the clicker become a legacy passed down to future canine companions. Just as you learned the language of clicker training, future dogs benefit from the knowledge you've acquired. The clicker becomes a timeless tool, bridging the communication gap for generations of dogs.

Clicker training is not just a personal journey but a shared experience. By sharing your insights and experiences, you contribute to a dog-lover community that embraces positive and effective training methods. When you share your success stories and challenges with fellow dog owners, the click can become a symbol of shared triumphs. It is a reminder that the collective wisdom of a community can enrich the journey.

The simplicity and effectiveness of clicker training make it a technique worth exploring for dog owners seeking a positive, rewarding, and harmonious relationship with their companions. With the click becoming the promise of a reward, this positive association becomes the avenue through which accelerated learning happens. The clicker training method aligns seamlessly with canine psychology. Dogs are natural learners; the clicker taps into their instinctive understanding of cause and effect. This method respects their cognitive abilities, making the training process engaging and enjoyable for both canine companions and their owners.

Whether you're teaching basic commands, complex tricks, or addressing behavioral challenges, clicker training is a versatile tool. Its adaptability allows you to tailor the training to your dog's individual needs and learning pace, making it suitable for dogs of all ages, breeds, and temperaments. Because it isn't really about the commands; it's about building a profound connection. Through the shared language of the click, you and your dog form a unique bond based on trust, cooperation, and mutual understanding. This strengthened bond extends beyond training sessions and enhances your overall relationship.

When faced with undesirable behaviors, clicker training offers a positive and effective approach to modification. Rather than focusing on punishment, this method redirects attention to reinforcing the desirable alternatives. It ultimately fosters a positive environment for learning and connection. This offers a refreshing departure from punitive methods. Instead of focusing on correction, dogs learn through the joy of receiving rewards instead. Their learning environment changes to one with an optimistic approach.

In the world of clicker training, every click is a note in the symphony of success, and the training journey is a timeless melody. Celebrating each victory, embracing the lifelong adventures it brings, and navigating the setbacks gracefully, the clicker becomes more than just a training tool- it becomes a conductor's baton, guiding the orchestra of your relationship with your dog. As you move through the training process, savor the clicks, relish in the victories, and remember that the experience is ever-evolving in the most magical of ways and will only deepen the connection between you and your faithful companion.

References

5 Humane dog training success stories. (2019, September 25). BC SPCA.

https://spca.bc.ca/news/animalkind-dog-training/

10 Dog Safety Tips for 2021 | Sit Means Sit Dog Training Raleigh. (2021, February 3).

Sitmeanssit.com. https://sitmeanssit.com/dog-training-mu/raleigh-dog-training/10-dog-safety-tips-for-2021/

AKC Canine Health Foundation. (n.d.). Www.akcchf.org. https://www.akcchf.org/canine-

health/your-dogs-health/caring-for-your-dog/getting-results-with-advanced.html

Assistance Dogs, Service Dogs, Emotional Support Dogs & Therapy Dogs. (n.d.). SunDog

Therapy. Retrieved November 2, 2023, from https://www.sundogtherapy.com/assistance-dogs/

Bindoff, A. (2012, March 1). *Karen Pryor Clicker Training.* Clickertraining.com.

https://www.clickertraining.com/how-to-teach-your-dog-left-and-right

Broitman, V. (2009, February 1). *The Life of One Clicker Trained Dog: A Love Story.*

Clickertraining.com. https://clickertraining.com/node/1014

Caldwell, A. (2017, October 27). *How to Train Your Dog to Bring You Something.*

Wagwalking.com.   https://wagwalking.com/training/bring-you-
          something

Class Clicker Techniques, Part One. (n.d.). Guide Dogs for the Blind.
          Retrieved November 2,

2023,   from   https://www.guidedogs.com/resources/client-
          resources/guide-dog-class-lecture-materials/class-clicker-
          techniques-part-
          one#:~:text=Your%20dog%20WILL%20stop%20action

CPDT-KA, P. M., CBCC-KA. (2001, March 30). Clicker Training and
          Trick Training Your Dog.

Whole   Dog   Journal.   https://www.whole-dog-
          journal.com/training/dog_training_behavior/clicker-training-
          and-trick-training-your-dog/

First aid for someone who is having a diabetic emergency. (n.d.). BRC Site Name.

https://www.redcross.org.uk/first-aid/learn-first-aid/diabetic-
          emergency

Frawley, E. (n.d.). Leerburg | The Power of Training Dogs with Markers.
          Leerburg.com.

https://leerburg.com/markers.htm

Gibeault, S. (2019, December 24). Clicker Training: Learn About Mark &
          Reward Dog Training

Using Clickers. American Kennel Club. https://www.akc.org/expert-
          advice/training/clicker-training-your-dog-mark-and-reward/

How to Teach Your Dog to Play Dead. (n.d.). MasterClass. Retrieved June 7,
          2021, from

https://www.masterclass.com/articles/how-to-teach-your-dog-to-play-
          dead

How to Treat Dog Nail Bleeding During Trimming. (n.d.). Wahl USA. Retrieved October 23,

2023, from https://wahlusa.com/expert-advice/grooming-pets/how-treat-dog-nail-bleeding-during-trimming#:~:text=A%20mix%20of%20cornstarch%20and

How to Use a Clicker for Dog Training: Tips & Tricks. (2021, September 24). The Dog Wizard.

https://thedogwizard.com/blog/how-to-use-a-clicker-for-dog-training/#:~:text=Using%20a%20clicker%20can%20communicate

Long, B. (2013, May 31). *Capture This! How to Put Your Dog's Cute Behaviors on Cue.*

American Kennel Club. https://www.akc.org/expert-advice/training/put-your-dogs-cute-behaviors-on-cue/

McLeod, S. (2023, September 11). *What is operant conditioning and how does it work?*

Simply Psychology. https://www.simplypsychology.org/operant-conditioning.html

Plonsky, M. (2015). *Goals for Beginning Obedience Class.* Www4.Uwsp.edu.

https://www4.uwsp.edu/psych/dog/LA/DrPBegObedGoals.htm

Plummer, S. (2017, October 26). *How to Train Your Dog to Run Through a Tunnel.*

Wagwalking.com. https://wagwalking.com/training/run-through-a-tunnel

Positive reinforcement training. (2023). The Humane Society of the United States.

https://www.humanesociety.org/resources/positive-reinforcement-training

Premaza, R. (2008, February 1). *Saving Jack: Clicker Training an Aggressive Border Collie.*

Clickertraining.com. https://www.clickertraining.com/node/1650

Pryor, K. (2015). *The Hidden History of Clicker Training.* Video.clickertraining.com.

https://video.clickertraining.com/programs/the-hidden-history-of-clicker-training

Rivers, B. (2021, November 1). *How to Teach a Dog to Roll Over.* ThatMutt.com.

https://www.thatmutt.com/how-to-teach-a-dog-to-roll-over/

Roth, C. (2022, July 18). *8 Dangerous Items Dogs Like to Chew.* PetsBest; Pet's Best Pet

Health Insurance. https://www.petsbest.com/blog/dangerous-items-dogs-chew#:~:text=It%20helps%20keep%20their%20teeth,intestinal%20tract%20that%20require%20surgery.

Stone, M. (2017, April 10). *How to Train Your Dog to Use a Potty Bell in Just Two Weeks.* Walk

and Wag. https://walkandwagchapelhill.com/how-to-train-your-dog-to-use-a-potty-bell-in-just-two-weeks/#:~:text=When%20it

Tricks to Teach Your Dog at Home: Crawl. (2023, January 24). Petco.

https://www.petco.com/content/petco/PetcoStore/en_US/pet-services/resource-center/behavior-training/Teach-Your-Dog-to-Crawl.html

Unsplash. (2017a, July 1). *Photo by Leio McLaren on Unsplash.* Unsplash.com.

https://unsplash.com/photos/person-sitting-on-rock-beside-of-brindle-through-sea-waves-crashing-on-rock-

WphP036Zuvg?utm_content=creditShareLink&utm_medium=
referral&utm_source=unsplash

Unsplash. (2017b, December 20). *Photo by Jakob Owens on Unsplash.* Unsplash.com.

https://unsplash.com/photos/gray-puppy-beside-red-ribbon-roll-
o0OnkkvJHrg?utm_content=creditShareLink&utm_medium=r
eferral&utm_source=unsplash

Unsplash. (2018a, February 18). *Photo by Oscar Sutton on Unsplash.* Unsplash.com.

https://unsplash.com/photos/woman-in-blue-denim-jacket-standing-
beside-short-coated-brown-dog-
bY5nz0STPC0?utm_content=creditShareLink&utm_medium=
referral&utm_source=unsplash

Unsplash. (2018b, March 28). *Photo by Eric Ward on Unsplash.* Unsplash.com.

https://unsplash.com/photos/photo-of-man-hugging-tan-dog-
ISg37AI2A-
s?utm_content=creditShareLink&utm_medium=referral&utm_
source=unsplash

Unsplash. (2019a, January 6). *Photo by Murilo Viviani on Unsplash.* Unsplash.com.

https://unsplash.com/photos/brown-and-white-dog-running-through-
pole-obstacles-
7wZxpC2oXYU?utm_content=creditShareLink&utm_medium
=referral&utm_source=unsplash

Unsplash. (2019b, April 14). *Photo by Alexandre Debiève on Unsplash.* Unsplash.com.

https://unsplash.com/photos/person-holding-white-short-coated-
dog-
SEX4KAz9ExQ?utm_content=creditShareLink&utm_medium
=referral&utm_source=unsplash

Unsplash. (2020a, February 15). *Photo by Andrea Lightfoot on Unsplash.* Unsplash.com.

https://unsplash.com/photos/black-white-and-brown-long-coated-dog-on-yellow-and-white-inflatable-ring-IrZ5xXXCsn4?utm_content=creditShareLink&utm_medium=referral&utm_source=unsplash

Unsplash. (2020b, September 6). *Photo by Destiny Wiens on Unsplash.* Unsplash.com.

https://unsplash.com/photos/white-and-brown-short-coat-medium-dog-on-green-grass-field-during-daytime-RIyGkwus3Po?utm_content=creditShareLink&utm_medium=referral&utm_source=unsplash

Unsplash. (2022, January 20). *Photo by Ayla Verschueren on Unsplash.* Unsplash.com.

https://unsplash.com/photos/a-table-topped-with-a-bowl-of-food-and-a-bowl-of-crackers-k4AGBfCz-I0?utm_content=creditShareLink&utm_medium=referral&utm_source=unsplash

Waggoner, C. (2009, May 1). *Loving Sasha: Clicker Training and a Canine Wheelchair.*

Clickertraining.com. https://www.clickertraining.com/node/2194

What Are the Different Types of Service Dogs? - UDS Foundation. (2020, February 15).

Udservices.org. https://udservices.org/types-of-service-dogs/

Printed in Great Britain
by Amazon